STRAPPED

Fighting for the soul of the
American working class

Michelle Teheux

Copyright © 2024 Michelle Teheux

All rights reserved

The characters and events portrayed in this book are fictitious. Any similarity to real persons, living or dead, is coincidental and not intended by the author.

No part of this book may be reproduced, or stored in a retrieval system, or transmitted in any form or by any means, electronic, mechanical, photocopying, recording, or otherwise, without express written permission of the publisher.

ISBN: 9798341175259

Printed in the United States of America

I dedicate this book to the memory of my talented and hard-working sister, Tracey Lynn Mueller Carlin.

You deserved so much more than the world gave you.

You were fabulous.

CONTENTS

Title Page
Copyright
Dedication

Foreword
Introduction
How the 'Bootstrap' Myth Weakens Workers	1
Suddenly, Everyone Is Courting the Working Class	8
Yes, We Know Free Stuff Isn't Free	12
Here's What They Really Mean When They Say Nobody Wants To Work Anymore	18
Why You Can't Afford Your Doctor, Dentist, Veterinarian or Even Dinner at Olive Garden	21
Here's Why Poor People Keep Voting Against Their Own Self Interest	27
What Capitalists Get Wrong About Human Motivation	33
Boomers: Worked. Gen X: Irked. Millennials: Shirked.	37
A Glut of Elites? No, It's Much Worse Than That	43
Why Are the Poor Still With Us?	49
Why 'Don't Spend Money You Don't Have' Is Dumb Advice	53
My Old Cast Iron Skillet Explains a Lot	61

This One is for All the Well-Educated, Cultured, Hard-Working Poor People	66
Poverty Isn't What It Used To Be	70
How Did We Decide Some Advantages Are Fair Game and Others Are Not?	75
Every Billionaire Is Mentally Ill	80
The Thing That Keeps Us Poor	84
It's Time To Burst That Bubble You're In	88
Lifestyle Creep Is Out To Get You	92
All You Grateful Laid-Off People On LinkedIn Need To Get Real	95
Workers Are the Real Philanthropists; Bezos, Gates and Musk Are Just Exploiters	99
Poor People and Rich People Live In Different Worlds	103
I Wonder What All The Poor People Are Doing Today?	109
The Dark Side of Heartwarming Stories	114
'Dirty Hands, Clean Money'	118
It's Just Money, People	122
Does Poverty Build Your Character?	125
We're Still Here, So There's That	128
About The Author	129
Praise For Author	131
Books By This Author	135

FOREWORD

Chances are good that you know something I don't right now. I'm writing this in the weeks before the 2024 presidential election and I have no idea who is going to win. If you're reading this after Nov. 5, 2024, you know what happened.

For a long time, the people in power have ignored the working class, but in this election cycle – and in the previous one – both parties started reaching out. Suddenly, everyone claims to care about the working class, but most of it is mere lip service.

Traditionally, the Democrats were the pro-union people and they thought that the working class would automatically stick with them forever, but President Ronald Reagan put a lot of effort into dismantling unions, and the movement of manufacturing jobs to other countries did the rest.

The Republicans didn't need to pay much attention to the working class to win them over. We'll talk more about this later.

The working and middle classes deserve better

This is a country in which about half the population is either in poverty or just a couple of paychecks away from landing there. That's an awful lot of people to write off as just not having worked hard enough to make it, and it's my hope that you'll keep that in mind as you read.

Most of the essays in this book originally ran on either Medium.com or in my Substack, *Untrickled*. I publish regularly on both platforms. I've adapted them to use here, but I'm writing more all the time. If you like what you're reading here, I invite you to find me in both places.

I also have a novel, *The Trailer Park Rules*, which uses fiction to illustrate how the system makes it harder for ordinary people to survive.

In my life, I've bounced between the working and middle class and thanks to my former career as a newspaper editor, I've met people who are homeless all the way up to the wealthy and powerful. This book is written from years of personal experience.

Those are my husband's boots on the cover, by the way. He wears them to work every day.

– Michelle Teheux
Friday, Sept. 13, 2024

INTRODUCTION

Feeling strapped for cash? Why don't you just lift yourself up by your own bootstraps? Go ahead, give it a try.

It's impossible, of course. Originally, people used that term sarcastically to describe an impossible task. It's odd that the meaning has now morphed into the opposite. (You'll read more about this in the first essay.)

Do you know what works better? A hand reaching out and offering you a lift.

Your effort is important, but so is getting some help from the people around you. Sometimes you're the one who needs a lift and sometimes you're the one in a position to lift someone up. People working together will always be able to accomplish more things than if everyone goes it alone.

It's not just you!

Do you feel like life is getting harder?

If you're working harder than your parents ever did but not doing as well, *it's not just you.*

If you have done everything society told you to do and are working your ass off but can't understand why you aren't getting anywhere, *it's not just you.*

And if you have started to question everything you've been told about the power of the individual to determine their own future, *it's not just you.*

I've been writing about this disconnect for years.

We stress the power of the individual. We tell you it's a free country, and if you don't manage to accomplish everything you want, *you must have done something wrong.*

I offer another view

If a teacher gives a test and 24 of her 25 students understand the material and score well, we can assume she taught effectively. Whatever went wrong with the one kid who failed was due to something else. But if 24 of the 25 students fail and only one kid passes, we are probably going to question that teacher's approach.

Society is the same way.

If only a few lazy people were broke but every hard worker was living well, we could blame the few. But that's not what's happening, is it?

Instead, roughly half of Americans earn so little they don't owe any federal income tax. (They're still paying plenty of other forms of tax.) The system is not set up to work for about half of us. That, I would say, is a problem.

Now, you might say half of Americans are just too lazy or stupid to succeed, but if you're a working-class or lower-middle class person – or even smack-dab in the middle of the middle class – look around. You certainly know plenty of hard workers who just can't get ahead.

Maybe you're one of them.

Have you ever gotten your vehicle stuck in snow or mud?

This probably happens at some point to every new driver, and it's very frustrating. You think you're going to be able to put the car in reverse, push the pedal to the metal, and pop yourself right out of the rut you're in.

But that's not the way it works. Instead, the harder you accelerate, the deeper your tires dig in. This is where the phrase "spinning your wheels" comes from. You're stuck until some other people come along to help give you a push, or until a tow truck pulls you free.

Sometimes, your own effort just is not enough.

There are times when you need a helping hand, and getting your car out of a rut is definitely one of those times. There are a lot of other times, too.

Would you insist you could drive your way out of the mud all by yourself? Or would you accept that you needed a push from someone?

You've been bombarded your whole life with the message that a determined person can accomplish everything

You've been told repeatedly that you can do anything that you set your mind to. You've been told that hard work and determination will lead to success. That's what your teachers and the media and everyone around you said.

You know who loves to make this claim?

I'll tell you who: People who had certain privileges that helped them on their way. They don't complain about how our system is set up. After all, it's worked just great for them.

This includes some people who were born into wealthy and/or well-connected families, but it also includes others who had some other lucky break. They were in the right place at the right time, or they happened to qualify for a certain scholarship. Maybe they married into a wealthy family or an early boss took a shine to them and helped them advance in their careers.

There's nothing wrong with any of those things. Any help any of us gets along the way is great! The problem is when someone begins to believe that because they've attained wealth, power and success, it means they're better or more deserving than others.

Sometimes they *are* better at their job. Sometimes they are not. And if you've been in the workplace for any length of time at all, you must have noticed that.

If you truly believe that everybody gets what they deserve in this life, you can write off everyone who isn't making it.

They had the same chance to make it as you did, but they just didn't work hard enough, or maybe they made dumb choices. Either way, they got what they deserved.

You can go off and drive your Lexus or whatever into the sunset, secure in the knowledge that the world is fair. You're doing great for a reason.

You. Are. Special.

"Blessed," even.
Yeah.

Whining doesn't get us anywhere

OK, so the world isn't fair. Who knew, right?

But you still have to work hard. You might have to work much harder than some people, even knowing your hard work may not get you as far as you deserve. (People of color have been saying for years that they have to work twice as hard to get half as far. I believe them.)

You won't get anywhere by sitting on your ass and complaining about this. I hope that's not what you've gotten from this so far. You can complain all you want if it makes you feel better – I do and it does, somewhat.

But you still have to work

If you want to start a business or take up a profession or create art or anything else, you're going to have to put in the hard work and make sacrifices. But that's not the whole story, no matter what anyone else claims.

The world is full of talented, hard-working people who struggle. Very few people are successful solely thanks to their own efforts.

No man is an island, John Donne said in 1624; this isn't a new idea. We don't operate independently – even though Americans love the idea of the independent person making things happen through their own determination.

It's our favorite fairy tale. But, like other fairy tales, it's not real life.

We all need other people

No matter how successful someone is, they can point to help they got along the way. They had at least one helping hand along the way, and perhaps several:
- Supportive teachers who saw something in them
- A loan officer who was willing to work with them
- Contacts who boosted them
- A business partner who joined forces with them

- Mentors who inspired them
- A family that supported them
- Friends who believed in them
- A scholarship that lifted them

I've been writing about this subject for a long time now, and it resonates with a lot of people. What a relief it is to understand, finally, that there are systemic problems that make it harder for each individual. Once we understand that, we can try to find workarounds.

Beware of survivorship bias

There is a formulaic story you've read many times and it goes like this: A writer/musician/actor or whatever makes a big splash and in interviews, says things like, *"I knew my hard work would eventually pay off. I believed in myself and I never gave up."*

Journalists love doing these stories. (I was a journalist for 30 years, so I know!) Who doesn't enjoy these inspiring accounts of how hardship and grit eventually yielded to glorious success?

Do you know what kind of stories journalists almost never do? They seldom interview the person who has been waiting tables by day and singing or doing comedy in clubs several nights a week, for decades, never giving up hope until they eventually die broke.

"Musician who believed in himself but never found success dies at 80" makes for a really bad headline.

Nobody knows how many people give up and take whatever job they can get or never give up and die in a cheap apartment somewhere. We only hear about the people who beat the odds. But you can bet there are a lot more people who don't make it than do. And some of those people were talented as hell but just never quite took off.

That's survivorship bias

And it's not just creators who struggle. It's also people whose dream is to start a roofing business or a restaurant. Or to go to law school and make partner at a big firm. Or to sell real estate. Or to get an MBA and land a lucrative job in big business. Everyone has a different dream.

Sometimes the hard work pays off and the dream comes true. But other times that doesn't happen, even if the person works very hard and seems to have done everything possible.

It's even harder for women

There's a reason fewer women than men are CEOs, and that reason is not that men are more talented or harder-working. Give me a break. Sexism is baked into the system.

We were told that women could *have* it all. The truth is that women are expected to *do* it all. You say you're having trouble raising the children and cooking and cleaning and running a company all at the same time?

Gosh, that's weird. Have you tried sleeping less?

There's a reason why people of color tend to make less money than white people, and that reason is not that white people are better workers. Racism is baked into the system, too.

I hop you don't go around telling people you aren't political

Be political! Join worthwhile movements. Pay attention, vote thoughtfully, and (if you can) write checks to charities and causes you believe in. A group chorus is louder than a solo voice.

Some of the problems vexing Americans have already been solved in other countries; I'm married to a European and as he says, there are some things better here and other things better there. If we stopped mindlessly chanting *"We're No. 1!"* and looked around, we would see some potential new ways of doing things.

Universal health care would be a big one. It works. We should do it. We waste hundreds of billions of dollars every year by refusing to fix our broken healthcare system that serves the insurance companies more than it does patients and healthcare professionals.

Stop thinking that all you can do is keep trying to make things happen on your own. Too many people spin their wheels as hard as they can their whole life, when what they need is five minutes with a damned tow truck. When you find someone willing and able to help you, thank them graciously.

Keep your eyes open for others who need a hand. Sometimes, it's a very small thing that makes a big difference. (Like five minutes with a tow truck.) You might offer professional guidance or agree to look over someone's resume or put in a good word with the HR people where you work. We aren't in this alone.

We are all living in this society together, and everything works better when we help each other.

Who is this book for?

This is not a self-help book that will offer you advice on how to be No. 1 despite the system. This is the opposite of a self-help book. This is a humankind-helping-each-other book.

My hope is that after you've read this book, you will feel better about yourself, regardless of whether you have reached some arbitrary idea of success or have found an alternate way to define it.

I also hope you'll find small ways to help others along the way if you can. And vote.

Or maybe you're absolutely killing it in life – I hope so! If that's you, perhaps this book will change your views about other people. I've seen this information open people's eyes and change their lives.

But mainly, I encourage you to think about our system in new ways. You have to learn how to hold these two views at the same time:

One, individuals are responsible for doing the best they can.

Two, our society/culture/government requires systemic change so it works better for everyone – not just the few at the top.

HOW THE 'BOOTSTRAP' MYTH WEAKENS WORKERS

The dark reason we insist individuals can overcome anything

We Americans sure do love our rags to riches myths.

This is the land of opportunity and anybody can succeed if they work hard enough. Just pull yourself up by your own bootstraps!

Did you know that originally the term "bootstrapping" was used sarcastically to describe an impossible task? Yet now, the meaning has morphed into the opposite.

I invite you to give it a try. First, put on a pair of boots with straps on the back. Next, reach back, grab those straps and pull yourself up. It didn't work? Huh. Maybe you need to pull a little harder.

Come on, man! You can do it!

Except of course it's literally impossible

There's a reason we tell people to pull themselves up by their own bootstraps even though we know it can't be done.

It's one of the ways people in power keep the rest of us from complaining that we're being screwed. We keep trying and trying and blaming ourselves when we have trouble. Of course we blame ourselves. Who else can we blame?

We know we sound like whiners and snowflakes if we protest

that we're trapped in an unfair system — and that's deliberate. Anytime there's a protest movement, it's dismissed as a bunch of lazy moochers who do not want to work.

If you favor a higher minimum wage, subsidized daycare, affordable college, universal health care or anything similar, you are not someone who wants a stronger society that works for more people. No, you are a dirty socialist who wants to steal the fruits of someone else's hard labor.

Most of us who want a better world have been working hard all our lives and we are proud of it. We are repulsed at the very idea of laziness and will do anything to avoid being slapped with such a label. So we put our heads down, suck it up and work a little harder.

The powerful love to cherry-pick outliers

There are, in fact, lots of inspiring and powerful stories about people who grew up in poverty or came to the U.S. with just a small amount of money in their pocket but somehow ended up very successful.

We tell the story of the one person who succeeded instead of the thousands who did not because we love to put the responsibility on the individual — and only the individual. In the 1800s, Horatio Alger made a fortune with his rags-to-riches fantasy stories that the public just ate up.

The modern versions of these stories are always presented as a guide for the rest of us: "This guy grew up in public housing and now he's the CEO of a multi-million-dollar company. If he can do it, you can do it!"

If Peter Piper plants a row of peppers in his garden but neglects to water them and only one of them thrives enough to produce peppers, do you assume all but one of the pepper plants were the problem?

I'd be inclined to conclude it was the lack of water. And I'd realize that if I wanted to pick a peck of peppers next time, I'd need to take better care of my garden.

I would not point to my lone pepper plant as clear evidence

against irrigation.

Our 'garden' is in trouble

We have neglected it. Our society doesn't care about the poor or working classes and barely worries about the shrinking middle class, which is why it's shrinking.

We have one lush, thriving corner of the garden on which we lavish most of our resources. The ultra-wealthy keep demanding lower and lower tax rates, justifying it with the claim that they are job creators.

The rest of society withers.

The real job creators, however, are the ordinary middle-class people who are purchasing goods and services. Enable more poor people to join the middle class and they'll happily spend more money buying homes and filling them up with furniture and — perhaps — even some kids.

The ultra-wealthy do not necessarily work harder than the rest of us. They are not necessarily smarter. We do not live in a meritocracy; we live in a winner-take-all system that protects the well-being of those who already have fortunes. Our tax system virtually ensures that the rich will get richer and the poor will get poorer.

The rich pay their pet lawmakers to keep it that way.

According to OXFAM International, the super-rich have claimed half of all new wealth in the past decade. French economist Thomas Piketty, author of Capital in the Twenty First Century, blames the way we tax wealth vs earned income for much of the inequality.

Spoiler: Anyone living on their investment income, including nepo babies who have never had a job, enjoys tax advantages over people working hard for their paychecks. If we'd set out to design an engine to drive income inequality, we could scarcely have come up with anything more effective than what we have.

We are living in a system that sets the non-rich up for failure, and then criticizes them for it. Meanwhile, more than half of Americans say they don't have enough money to cover a $1,000 emergency.

Are all men created equal?

If we believe that, then why do we treat people so unequally? There's little evidence the Founding Fathers really meant what they said. They cared about white male landowners, mostly. They were not talking about Black people (or any non-white people) or any women. They didn't care much about poor white men without property, either.

As for our right to the pursuit of happiness, well, we provide a smooth path for some and a rocky one for others.

It's incredibly condescending and a great example of toxic positivity to tell the working and middle classes that they have the same opportunities to succeed as the monied class.

We had two choices

We could organize our society so that everyone had reasonably equal opportunities to succeed or we could smooth the path for certain groups of people and then convince everyone else that we had faith in their ability to overcome every difficulty.

You know which one we chose.

The Washington Post has a famous piece, *Poor kids who do everything right don't do better than rich kids who do everything wrong*. It clearly shows just how much we do not have a meritocracy.

It's not just a matter of money and professional success, though

It's about how we organize so many things in our society. We are set up to fail and then blamed for our failure.

Did you know people who live in walkable neighborhoods are less likely to be obese than those who do not? You'd think we might take that information and redesign neighborhoods accordingly, but instead, we simply blame the residents of poor neighborhoods — those are usually the non walkable places — for being obese.

Did you know people who live near each other but in different zip codes can have dramatically different life expectancies? You can plug your address into a calculator provided by the Robert Wood Johnson Foundation and see how your zip code affects your longevity.

I entered my address and the address of someone I know in a wealthier area less than 15 miles away from me. I'm frankly stunned by the difference; according to that calculator, living where I do will cost me five years off my life.

We could attempt to provide better outcomes for the people in the poorer zip codes, but we don't. Those people should just move.

Have you ever wondered why we are fine with junk food companies doing everything they can to convince people (including children!) to ingest their crap while we blame anyone who overindulges in it for making bad choices?

Why do we allow Big Pharma to convince ordinary people with no medical backgrounds that they need to start taking a certain drug? (Only the U.S. and New Zealand allow this.)

We know that payday loan places charge the unbanked as much as 400 percent, but instead of outlawing this practice, we merely shrug and say poor people should make better choices.

It's a gross mischaracterization of our cherished ideals of freedom and personal responsibility, reworked to suit the needs of the exploitation class:

You have the freedom to make good choices, just as corporations have the freedom to do everything possible to convince you to make bad choices, and in the end we'll reward them and blame you.

Sources:

Useless Etymology
The Origins of the Phrase 'Pull Yourself Up By Your Bootstraps'
https://uselessetymology.com/2019/11/07/the-origins-of-the-phrase-pull-yourself-up-by-your-bootstraps/

TIME Magazine

Horatio Alger Is a Hoax, But We Can Still Celebrate the American Dream
https://time.com/6305543/horatio-alger-myth-american-dream/

OXFAM International
Richest 1% bag nearly twice as much wealth as the rest of the world put together over the past two years
https://www.oxfam.org/en/press-releases/richest-1-bag-nearly-twice-much-wealth-rest-world-put-together-over-past-two-years

Thomas Piketty
Capital in the Twenty-First Century
https://www.amazon.com/Capital-Twenty-Century-Thomas-Piketty/dp/067443000X

Bankrate
Bankrate's 2024 Annual Emergency Savings Report
https://www.bankrate.com/banking/savings/emergency-savings-report/

The Washington Post
Poor kids who do everything right don't do better than rich kids who do everything wrong
https://www.washingtonpost.com/news/wonk/wp/2014/10/18/poor-kids-who-do-everything-right-dont-do-better-than-rich-kids-who-do-everything-wrong/

Boston University School of Health
U.S. Neighborhood Walkability Influences Physical Activity, BMI Levels
https://www.bu.edu/sph/news/articles/2023/us-neighborhood-walkability-influences-physical-activity-bmi-levels/#:~:text=They%20found%20that%20adults%20who,in%20neighborhoods%20with%20low%20walkability.

Robert Wood Johnson Foundation
What Makes A Long Life?

https://www.rwjf.org/en/insights/our-research/interactives/whereyouliveaffectshowlongyoulive.html

JAMA Network
Association Between Drug Characteristics and Manufacturer Spending on Direct-to-Consumer Advertising
https://jamanetwork.com/journals/jama/fullarticle/2801060#:~:text=The%20US%20and%20New%20Zealand,consumer%20advertising%20for%20prescription%20drugs.

Consumer Financial Protection Bureau
What is a payday loan?
https://www.consumerfinance.gov/ask-cfpb/what-is-a-payday-loan-en-1567/

SUDDENLY, EVERYONE IS COURTING THE WORKING CLASS

The demographic everybody ignored is being noticed now

Lately, I've felt like the girl who couldn't get a date to prom but is now being ardently courted by the captains of the football and basketball teams.

Until recently, everyone ignored the working class. The Democrats took us for granted. Who else were poor and lower-middle-class folks going to vote for? The rich-loving Republicans? Ha.

But then the Republicans – the people most responsible for keeping down the poor and poor-adjacent in the first place – began scrounging around for votes and discovered there was a giant group of people who felt ignored by the Democratic party. And they scooped them right up.

The Dems regularly talked about doing things to benefit the non-rich – subsidized daycare, a better Earned Income Tax Credit, stronger unions, universal healthcare, student loan reform, etc. – but little of this ever came to fruition. That hasn't always been their fault, of course. The regressive party has been very good at preventing progress.

But still – ask a truck driver what the Dems have done for him lately, and you are not going to like his answer.

You know what that guy does know, however?

The popular perspective is that the Dems are cultural elites who care more about LGBTQ folks and racial minorities than they do people driving forklifts or picking up garbage (even though plenty of people of color and LGBTQ people do such work!) Furthermore, the blue party is unpatriotic and wants to get rid of all the cops.

You and I know that's inaccurate and unfair, but that's not the message the working class hears. It's hard to fight against the highly emotional messaging the GOP sends out.

If you imagine a Democrat reading aloud a dense policy statement and a Republican flashing a meme, you won't be far off.

I regularly shake my head at the memes I see people from my red hometown post on social media. They think President Joe Biden opened the border and invited immigrants to come right in, and then he gave them a free house. (Seriously, some people think that.)

They fervently believe the country is full of lazy people who don't work but who have higher incomes than they do. They're upset when players take a knee during the Pledge of Allegiance at sporting events. They are convinced the Democrats are just seconds away from seizing all their guns.

For years, I tried to change minds

I posted citations. I explained I'm married to a legal immigrant and the process is very different from what they imagine. I reminded them that in eight years, President Barack Obama did not take their guns even once, nor did Biden.

I have heard so many lower-income Americans complain about their high income taxes, when the truth is that they're paying little or no income taxes at all. They are, however, paying high payroll taxes and not everyone understands the difference.

I don't think my facts ever convinced anybody. You cannot use logic and facts to change someone's mind if their opinion was never based on fact in the first place. No citation hits harder than a meme that gives people the feels. I finally had to give up.

To return to the dating metaphor, when your best friend is gaga over an abusive boyfriend, listing his faults almost never convinces her to break up with him. Not when he's whispering to her all the comforting lies she wants to hear.

The Democrats used to gain strong support from unions, but President Ronald Reagan helped break them up. Now Dems feel more like the party of educated professionals. Some working class people feel distrustful of them and view them as elites. When Democrats say, *"Let's make college affordable for all,"* some working class people hear, *"Let's let kids run up huge bills learning useless crap and make the hardworking taxpayers cover the cost."*

Here again is a belief that needs to be busted: There are, in fact, lots of educated people in the working, lower and middle classes.

I'm raising my hand here and waving it around. Here I am! I have a college degree, have worked many professional jobs and have never surpassed $40K per year in my life. I know many others like me.

When you think "working class," you're probably thinking of unionized men in factories, but you need to expand your vision. Think nursing home aides. Think cashiers. Think low-level office jobs in which people are nicely dressed but poorly paid. Think of people who have never worked for a union and thus don't understand what a union could do for them.

Former President Donald Trump hurt the working class badly, even as they flocked to him. The working class is often unaware of the various useful measures the Democrats have put in place or the many others they tried to put in place. Democrats don't know how to get their message out. We try to talk about facts instead of emotions, and it seldom works that way.

The working class isn't stupid

But they are often uninformed. I blame the media for that.

The media does a poor job of telling the real story, and the real story is often complicated and would require significant background information to be understood.

A great deal of the pain suffered by the bottom half of

America has to do with complicated stories it's not easy to tell. Deregulated business. Monopolies. Hedge funds. Private equity. Pharmacy benefit managers. A tax structure that benefits the wealthy. Citizens United. A beaten-down press – yes, the press is both victim and villain in this story. Social media algorithms that elevate comfortable untruths that make some people feel better.

Of course, the other classes are just as uninformed. I once heard an educated, wealthy business owner and Trump supporter explain to me that while the economy always does better under Democrats, that's because every change shows up only when the following administration takes power.

Therefore, he patiently explained to me, anything good that happens while a Democratic president is in office is due to the actions taken by the previous Republican, and anything bad that happens during a Republican administration is directly attributable to what the previous Democratic president did.

I wish I were making this up.

It isn't just the working class that's clueless. Please understand they are no more clueless than any other demographic. For proof, I offer Elon Musk and all the other rich, educated, ignorant Trump supporters. There are many. And you can't blame their lack of education or opportunities for their incomprehensible choice.

But there's some hope

The Dems' messaging now is better than any I've seen in a long time, perhaps ever. Yes, MAGA is weird! No, we won't go back!

You could hardly come up with a better message for conservatives than "Make America Great Again." It harkens back to a mythical time when things were better.

"We are not going back" could not be more brilliant. It reminds us of the direction we want to go – forward, not backward.

And it works for every single American.

YES, WE KNOW FREE STUFF ISN'T FREE

The U.S. lives in an alternate reality of its own

Each time anyone voices support for universal healthcare or any other social benefit, another person will immediately jump in to say this: "Free stuff isn't free!"

You know when we never hear that?
When we talk about things like public roadways, the national defense or even local things like police and fire.

We understand that some things benefit all of us and so all of us need to pay into them. It's not very controversial to say that a city on a river requires a bridge. Nobody screams, *"If you people want to cross that river so bad, you just need to get your ass into the water and swim!"*

Even in the case of public schools, which do come with plenty of controversy, very few people call for outright closure. They might grumble about free school lunches or a curriculum they don't like, but almost nobody thinks we should stop educating the public.

So it's a matter of hashing out what stuff we think society as a whole should make sure is available for all, and what things we think individuals should pay for if they want them.

I'm married to a European man
Because I have many European in-laws and friends, I'm more familiar than most Americans about how differently things work

in other countries.

Each time I visit the Netherlands, where my husband is a citizen, I have the same exact thought: "Why can't Americans have nice things like this?"

It's like stepping into an alternate reality — one in which the far-right did not squash all progressive ideas.

Things that seem like pipe dreams in the U.S. — health care for all, a comfortable work-life balance, unions that look out for workers, generous paid parental leave, smarter energy programs, solid social safety nets, compassionate care for the elderly, healthier food, convenient public transportation and a million other things — are taken for granted in places like the Netherlands.

Systems and individuals

It isn't that the Dutch don't have any problems. Of course they do. But they seem to assume that one role of government is to set up systems in such a way that citizens' lives are better.

In the U.S., there is no such assumption. It's every man for himself here. Do several million of you think the system isn't working well for you? Well, several million of you will need to figure out individually how to get by as best you can. We will not change the system.

The Dutch have multiple right-wing, central and far-left parties. After every election, the winning candidates have to form a coalition and work together.

The U.S. has two main parties: The far-right Republican party and the center-right Democrat party. By international standards, the Democrats are not liberal at all, let alone socialist or communist as some ill-informed far-right Americans claim. There's little hashing things out. It's more of a winner-take-all. Never mind what 49.9 percent of the population wants — they get nothing. The spoils go to the 50.1 percent who won.

Or, in the case of the presidency, the minority will repeatedly be able to grasp power over the wishes of the majority via the Electoral College.

Healthcare is a great example of what this has led to

I've made it a point to ask many Europeans how they feel about their healthcare. So far, every single person I've asked has had good things to say about the quality of their care and the cost.

Can you name even one American who can say the same?

Americans don't agree about very much, but we do come together on this. Bring up this subject at any gathering and everyone is eager to tell their story about waiting forever to see a specialist, about being billed a fortune for something simple or about someone they know who went bankrupt after a serious illness.

There's a 'but'

But, they'll add, other countries pay so much higher taxes.

This is true.

The U.S. has generally lower taxes than other well-off countries. According to the Tax Policy Center of the Urban Institute and the Brookings Institution, citizens of Denmark pay the highest taxes. The French are in second place. The U.S. is way down in 32nd place.

However, when you take into consideration what Americans pay annually in health insurance — and what their employer pays — plus what they pay out of pocket because their health insurance doesn't cover everything — it's certain that most of us would be money ahead with some form of universal healthcare. (The exact system varies by country, but in general everyone is covered either "free" or for an affordable cost.)

Because everyone's situation is different and the cost of health insurance, healthcare and taxes vary considerably by countless factors, it's impossible to nail down an exact number. My health insurance costs and medical bills are no doubt quite different from yours, and so is my tax bill.

Of course, different countries use tax dollars in different ways. Many countries provide lengthy paid maternity and paternity leaves, plus free or heavily subsidized healthcare, daycare and college, for example, plus of course all the usual costs of running a country that you'd expect taxes to cover.

American healthcare is generally inferior yet more expensive

You've probably heard people claim that in other countries, you have to wait to see a specialist. That's hardly limited to other countries.

An older American I know just waited six months to see a cardiologist!

The U.S. pays more for its healthcare than any other country. Per capita, we pay $12,318. In second place is Germany, at $7,383, according to the World Economic Forum.

This might be somewhat acceptable if we at least had the best healthcare in the world for this high cost.

We do not.

The University of Michigan School of Public Health notes that even though we're paying a lot, our outcomes are worse.

We have the lowest life expectancy at birth

We also have the highest maternal and infant mortality, according to The Commonwealth Fund. These are well-accepted measures of how well a country's healthcare system is functioning, and we're failing.

The Lancet is one of our most reputable medical journals. In Improving the prognosis of health care in the USA, the authors calculate that "a single-payer, universal health-care system is likely to lead to a 13% savings in national health-care expenditure, equivalent to more than U.S $450 billion annually...."

That study notes that the entire system would cost less than employers, households and governments spend now, and would save 1.73 million human life-years every year compared with what we're doing now.

World Health Systems Facts, a project of the Real Reporting Foundation, provides a nice comparison of costs and life expectancy by country, along with plenty of useful information.

Why would we not choose to implement a system that saves us money and keeps us healthier?

There's a simple explanation: Americans are always afraid that somebody somewhere might get a benefit they did not work hard enough for. Many Americans would prefer to keep a wasteful and costly system that results in worse outcomes to avoid that.

Better that people go bankrupt and die prematurely than implement a system that will just give away free goodies like birth, knee replacements, chemotherapy and appendectomies. Or even yearly checkups, for that matter. I mean, can you imagine all the people lining up to have their healthy gallbladders removed if you could just have it done for free anytime you wanted?

It's easy to make the case for providing universal health care. All the numbers speak for themselves. I think the same arguments apply to an awful lot of things that all of society benefits from but that not everyone can afford to access.

That's not socialism or communism. It's just setting up systems that work so people can thrive.

Sources:

Tax Policy Center
Urban Institute and Brookings Institution
https://www.taxpolicycenter.org/briefing-book/how-do-us-taxes-compare-internationally

World Economic Forum
Charted: The countries with the most expensive healthcare
https://www.weforum.org/agenda/2023/02/charted-countries-most-expensive-healthcare-spending/

School of Public Health, University of Michigan
Health and Taxes: Why People around the World Are Healthier than Americans
https://sph.umich.edu/pursuit/2019posts/health-and-taxes-040919.html

The Commonwealth Fund
U.S. Health Care from a Global Perspective, 2022: Accelerating Spending, Worsening Outcomes
https://www.commonwealthfund.org/publications/issue-briefs/2023/jan/us-health-care-global-perspective-2022

The Lancet
Improving the prognosis of health care in the USA
https://www.thelancet.com/journals/lancet/article/PIIS0140-6736(19)33019-3/abstract#:~:text=Taking%20into%20account%20both%20the,US%24450%20billion%20annually%20(based

World Health Systems Facts
Current Health Expenditure Per Capita and Average Life Expectancy at Birth
https://healthsystemsfacts.org/?gad_source=1&gclid=Cj0KCQjw3vO3BhCqARIsAEWblcDlvOTTJ8UF1-Q2P9BIa6sYM4-d2pwvnVCbc4x9HneMm8DMAguHN74aAqFFEALw_wcB

HERE'S WHAT THEY REALLY MEAN WHEN THEY SAY NOBODY WANTS TO WORK ANYMORE

Take note of who keeps saying this

I keep hearing people tell me nobody wants to work anymore. The people who say this, however, are invariably people who have had the same good jobs for years — or are retired.

I have yet to hear this claim from anybody who has dealt with a bout of unemployment in the last few years.

The unemployment rate is historically low

But it doesn't count people who settled for a part-time job or who switched to gig work or self-employment.

That would include people like me. I thought I'd work full-time until I was around 70, but it's tough to land a job when you're 50-plus. Almost every woman my age I know is unemployed, underemployed or doing some kind of gig or freelance work.

I'm sure there are exceptions, especially people who have highly specialized skills. I imagine 50-something doctors, for example, are much better off than people in non-tech fields.

A long-retired acquaintance threw out the "nobody wants to work anymore" claim to me recently, and when I pushed back, he said he could have a job in two hours if he wanted one. I'd like to see him manage it, frankly. He might be surprised how few jobs there are for elderly men.

When you can't find a full-time job, hearing people confidently claim that nobody wants to work anymore is particularly galling.

Job searches are not what they used to be

If you haven't been subjected to this torture in the last few years, you can't imagine how much things have changed. Some people, especially those who haven't job hunted for a decade, think you can walk into a workplace, ask to see the manager and simply wow them with your can-do attitude:

"Wow, I love your positive perspective! I definitely want you on the team! Can you start Monday? And is $100,000 to start OK?"

You can't apply in person even at most fast-food places now. You have to go online to apply. You aren't going to impress a manager by walking in and demonstrating how incredible you are.

I think the nobody-wants-to-work-anymore folks think people without jobs are holding out for cushy executive positions and need to suck it up and accept whatever they can get.

Once you've had a higher-level job, though, nobody wants to hire you for something they feel you're overqualified for. And even if they do hire you, they will likely restrict your hours to part-time so they don't have to pay you benefits.

I remember a few years ago an executive-level woman was desperate to flee a toxic workplace. She told me she erased much of her experience in order to try to land an entry-level job as a bank teller. She didn't get it.

And this was before the pandemic. It has not gotten better since then.

I'll be honest, I didn't even apply for anything entry-level

I knew it was futile to go the overqualified route. Besides, I worked many such jobs as a student, and I know how such workers are treated. My work ethic is stronger than that of most people I've worked with, but I'm not going to be told when I can use the restroom or get a drink of water. I don't think anybody should be treated that way, actually.

When they say nobody wants to work, what they mean is nobody wants to work at shitty jobs where they know they will be treated poorly.

I didn't hold out for top jobs. I applied for positions for which I was well qualified. It's not that I held out for something with high pay — I just wanted to do good work at a job I enjoyed.

This is why I freelance now

If I could land a full-time job that uses my writing, editing and communications skills, that would be great.

But I'm focusing my time and attention on opportunities that I have control over. I figure out what I want to do and find a way to learn the skills I need to do it. I've never had an employer teach me as many new skills as I've learned on my own in the past few years!

I'm incredibly proud of the things I've accomplished independent of any employer. But it makes me sad that I've had to go it alone.

WHY YOU CAN'T AFFORD YOUR DOCTOR, DENTIST, VETERINARIAN OR EVEN DINNER AT OLIVE GARDEN

Inflation isn't the whole explanation

When I was in college and making $3.35 per hour, I was able to pay the full cost of neutering my kitten, Putter. I also paid a dentist to fill a painful cavity around that time. I recall writing checks for both of these things.

A person with very little money could afford things like that then. Now, things have changed. Why? We talk about inflation and lagging pay, but that's not the whole story.

The vet I went to had her own private practice

It was a little small-town office. It wasn't fancy but it was pleasant. I remember it well almost four decades later. I didn't just pay for Putter to lose his boy bits — I also had to have some of his teeth pulled and he had to start taking pills for his epilepsy. That kitty had issues that I'd struggle to pay for now. But vet care was far more affordable then.

I only saw that dentist one time. There wasn't money in my budget for regular dental care, but I did need to have that cavity dealt with. I randomly picked a dentist from the yellow pages, got my painful tooth fixed and paid for it with the proceeds of my minimum wage job.

When I went to the doctor as a kid, it was always one doctor with his own office. (Yes, they were always men in those days. I am talking about the past right now. Some things were better and some things were worse.)

But now, when I visit a veterinarian, doctor or dentist, I'm not just paying for their professional services. I also have to help some private equity or hedge fund make an absolute killing.

No more do you go see Dr. Davis when you have a cavity; you go to something like Northside Dental Group, and you might never see the same dentist twice. Thanks, private equity! A piece in *The White Coat Investor* explains what private equity has done to dentistry. Private equity can extract value from a practice faster than your dentist can extract a wisdom tooth.

You don't go to Dr. Kim when you get a new kitten; you go to Best Friends Vet Clinic, and you'll see whatever vet is on duty when you get there. A piece in *The Atlantic* tells you how private equity has been gobbling up private veterinary practices the way my dog gobbles up table scraps.

You probably do have a specific doctor, and sometimes you will even see that doctor, if you set up an appointment in advance. But if you get sick, you'll see whatever doctor or nurse practitioner is there that day. *The Hill* explains it all. What private equity does to medical offices is akin to what the proctologist does after telling you to relax.

Opening your own private practice of any kind is expensive and daunting. I can well understand why a recent graduate, already loaded down with student debt, would decide to join a practice rather than renting an office, buying equipment, hiring help and all the rest.

Money trumps professional care

Everybody has to answer to their corporate overlords. When I have a medical appointment now, I feel like a product being hustled down the assembly line as quickly as possible. It's been ages since I've had a medical visit in which I wasn't made to feel like I was rudely taking up too much of my provider's time.

A *Wall Street Journal* piece details how some eye doctors feel pressured by their non-doctor bosses to perform far more eye surgeries in a day than they feel comfortable doing. In the *New York Times*, veterinarians at private equity practices say they are pressured to increase the "cost per client" or see as many as 21 animals per day.

I've been upsold at dental and vet appointments and I do not like it. I am paying for their professional expertise, and I should be able to trust them. But now, I always question whether the treatment being recommended is necessary and helpful or just profitable.

People who become doctors, dentists, veterinarians, pharmacists, etc. presumably chose their career because they wanted to provide professional care and they expected to make a comfortable living doing so. People who work in private equity don't care about the quality of care for the businesses they acquire, and they don't just want a comfortable living. They want to make a fortune.

It's not just the care professions

It's everything. A story in the *Harvard Business Review* talks about private equity firms finding ways to improve businesses' "performance." As an example, it says, "since taking Toys 'R' Us private in 2005, KKR, Bain Capital, and Vornado Realty Trust have had to replace the entire top management team and develop a whole new strategy for the business."

That "whole new strategy" they came up with explains why it's so hard to buy toys for my grandchildren now. The plunderers closed all the Toys 'R' Us stores in 2018, although they're now attempting to stage a comeback.

You can see asset-stripping in the restaurant world, too. A story in *Salon* explains how a hedge fund complained that Olive

Garden was in trouble for giving away too many breadsticks. That might sound halfway believable if, like me, you ever took growing teenagers there and watched them put away basket after basket of free breadsticks.

But the real issue was more along the lines of forcing Olive Garden to sell the real estate it sits on and then rent it back at punishingly high rates. That strategy doesn't make sense, of course, if you want to keep the restaurant open. It makes lots of sense if you want to extract as much money as you can as quickly as you can and don't care whether the business survives.

I used to be the editor of a daily newspaper owned by a hedge fund. Each time I had to cut a corner that I didn't want to cut, I died inside a little bit more. I, as editor, was not able to decide how to allocate resources, and I was not provided with the funds I needed to do the job right. (A character who works as a reporter in my novel *The Trailer Park Rules* lives through a similar hell.)

All I wanted to do was bring the public the news. I assume what I felt is very much like the feelings of someone who wants to take care of animals or people or just serve people affordable Italian food.

What do private equity and hedge funds do besides extract money from people who are trying to accomplish something good? So many children dream of growing up to be a vet. Or a doctor. Maybe even running a restaurant. I dreamed of being a reporter. Were some kids dreaming of extracting wealth from others no matter how much mayhem and pain they caused?

The uninformed public simply blames inflation and greed. But don't blame professionals for the high cost of care. They aren't keeping all that money you just paid them. Some investors who have never cared for anyone but themselves sure are tucking it away, though.

Sources:

Forage

Hedge Fund vs. Private Equity: What's the Difference?
https://www.theforage.com/blog/careers/hedge-fund-vs-private-equity#:~:text=Private%20 equity%20forms%20 typically%20 invest,stocks%2C%20options%2C%20and%20futures.

The White Coat Investor
The DSO Down-Low: How Private Equity Has Infiltrated Dentistry
https://www.whitecoatinvestor.com/dso-private-equity-dentistry/

The Atlantic
Why Your Vet Bill Is So High
https://www.theatlantic.com/ideas/archive/2024/04/vet-private-equity-industry/678180/

The Hill
Private equity is buying up health care, but the real problem is why doctors are selling
https://thehill.com/opinion/healthcare/4365741-private-equity-is-buying-up-health-care-but-the-real-problem-is-why-doctors-are-selling/

The Wall Street Journal
Dominant Eye Surgery Chain LasikPlus Put Profits Over Patient Care, Some Doctors Say
https://www.wsj.com/articles/dominant-eye-surgery-chain-lasikplus-put-profits-over-patient-care-some-doctors-say-11637247935

The New York Times
Why You're Paying Your Veterinarian So Much
https://www.nytimes.com/2024/06/23/health/pets-veterinary-bills.html

Harvard Business Review
The Strategic Secret of Private Equity
https://hbr.org/2007/09/the-strategic-secret-of-private-equity

Salon
The real Olive Garden scandal: Why greedy hedge funders suddenly care so much about breadsticks
https://www.salon.com/2014/09/17/the_real_olive_garden_scandal_why_greedy_hedge_funders_suddenly_care_so_much_about_breadsticks/

HERE'S WHY POOR PEOPLE KEEP VOTING AGAINST THEIR OWN SELF INTEREST

An explanation for liberals who don't get it

If you are living on beans, rice and the tomatoes from your garden, and you see someone else at the grocery store use a SNAP card to pay for a cart full of treats you can't afford, there's no way you aren't going to feel like a chump.

This explains why some working-class people hate welfare. These folks are working their tails off but not necessarily living better than people on assistance. When you're trying your ass off and sweating the rent, and you know somebody else who gets to live in public housing for almost nothing, there's some room for resentment there.

I've been that person keeping a running total of how much my groceries were going to cost, and putting back a few things sometimes to make sure I had enough money to pay for it all. Food stamps would have helped a lot, but I never quite qualified for them. And yes, seeing others use their benefits to purchase things I couldn't afford rankled. I'm not going to deny it.

Despite this, I've always believed in the need for a robust safety net with no shame, because I understand the root causes of poverty have at least as much to do with our system as with personal choices. I always understood, when I was at my brokest, that my financial issues were not of my own making.

That's the opposite of what we are taught to believe. You can do everything society tells you to do and still not have enough money, which is a message everyone needs to start understanding. In such cases, blaming yourself for your lack of money is like blaming yourself for winter.

The working poor hate welfare

Some of them hate it more than the wealthy do. You'd think it would be the other way around, right? You'd assume a poor person would realize how close they are to needing that assistance themselves. But in my experience, people who struggle to pay their own way take great pride in managing to do so, and feel real anger at the people who don't. They need to believe in the power of individuality. It's all they've got.

This is something your average middle-class white liberal doesn't understand. I think you have to be a working class liberal to be able to understand the nuances here.

If you are an educated white liberal who rolls your eyes at all the poor people voting against their own interests, and if you wonder why they fail to appreciate all the help Democrats are trying to give them through social programs, this is what you are missing.

Well-off conservatives also disapprove of welfare, but for different reasons. Most rich people move in circles where it's believed that hard work always leads to success. It doesn't, of course, but it's easy to believe that when everybody you personally know seems to be doing fine.

These people usually don't understand that their membership in a bubble of well-off people acts as a safety net. If they lose their job, they have the connections to get another and enough resources on hand to prevent them from losing everything in the meantime. If you're in the Upper Middle Class Club, valuable contacts come free with your membership. The members of that club have no idea how different life is for people outside it.

Welfare outrage

So far, all these attitudes make a certain kind of sense, but there's one more category that is very hard to understand: the welfare recipients who are outraged about welfare.

I have known many people who are utterly dependent upon some form of assistance but vocal about their hatred of it. And I don't mean vocal as in, *"I'm upset that I have no choice but to accept welfare in my situation"* but *"I'm furious that welfare exists at all."*

I've adjusted a few details to anonymize three such people I know.

Gail, the single mom in public housing

I blocked Gail from my social media during the Obama administration. I just couldn't take her frequent online rants about welfare recipients anymore, given the fact that she and her teenage daughter lived in public housing and neither worked.

The last I knew, she had attended nursing school at no charge, but had not finished her degree so continued to depend on assistance to live. Maybe she's found a way to finish and has a good job now. I hope so.

She was never able to understand she was exactly the same as all those people she vilified.

Roy and his large family on the medical card

Roy and his wife had a new baby every couple of years, and eventually they couldn't all fit into one vehicle. A kind man actually gave them a van large enough to seat the entire family.

Roy was vehemently against any kind of universal healthcare. *"When everybody has healthcare, nobody will have healthcare,"* is, as best as I can remember years later, a direct quote of Roy's. But Roy's family didn't have to pay for healthcare because they qualified for the medical card.

I was paying for my own family's health insurance and contributing my tax dollars to help pay for the care of people like Roy's family at that time — and was happy to do so, because I don't want anyone to go without healthcare. I found that ironic. I don't think that irony ever crossed Roy's mind.

Roy was quite open about all the various programs that his family benefitted from. His wife took their children to receive free lunches from the township each day during the summer when free school lunches were not available, for example. You would think someone like Roy would support the idea of universal health care and various assistance programs, since he and his wife could not support their large family without them.

But you would be wrong.

Tom, the disabled and judgy man

Tom suffers from several serious health problems and has not worked in years — nor should he. If I listed all his diagnoses, you'd agree he needs to prioritize his health.

I've listened to Tom speak derisively of "Obamacare" and "Obamaphones," both of which he personally depends on. I've known Tom's family for years, and I know how conservative and wealthy they are. His family could easily support him if they chose to. That would relieve him of the need to depend on the various assistance programs they all hate so much.

I haven't seen Tom for a while, but as far as I know, he still depends on some form of assistance to live. I think the need to take care of people like Tom is a pretty good argument for the existence of welfare. Maybe he's seen the light and no longer speaks out against it now, but I doubt it.

The myth of the welfare queen

You probably remember that President Ronald Reagan spun a story about welfare queens living it up at taxpayer expense. With a few exceptions — because there will always be somebody trying to game the system — people who depend on welfare don't have enough to live on. They generally have to use food pantries, secretly accept some help from their family, pick up and cash in aluminum cans, do some babysitting off the books or find some other strategy to survive.

They aren't enjoying cushy lives. Most would actually prefer to work, if they could find a job that would cover their basic living expenses.

Decades ago, I knew a single mom just a few years older than I was who kept trying to get off welfare. When I met her, we were working in the same restaurant, but I was a senior in high school and she was already divorced with two children.

Again and again, she'd get a job and start saving money, but the long arms of the poverty monster kept reaching out and dragging her back down into the pit. When you're just barely managing to feed your children, any illness, rent increase or car trouble is enough to throw you off. She finally managed it once she got remarried — because her new husband supported her and paid her tuition so she could get the job training that led to a decent job.

It would have made a lot of sense for society to have offered that kind of help to her years earlier. It actually would have saved taxpayer money and allowed her to start contributing to society much sooner.

Give back the Obamaphone, Tom!

Part of me regrets not having said, *"But Gail, you yourself depend on this program. Why are you so against it?"* Or, *"Roy, if you hate government-paid healthcare so much, why do you accept the medical card?"* Or, *"Tom, shouldn't you give back that Obamaphone that you are so angry exists?"*

I don't know how they'd react, but I suspect they would have become angry at me for not understanding that they are obviously nothing like those other welfare recipients. All those other welfare recipients are bad and lazy. Not them!

Gail, Roy and Tom are all white. I have a terrible suspicion about the relevance of that.

We do this on the state level, too

I've heard so many people in red states express anger about the blue states, not realizing that red states tend to receive more money from the federal government than they paid in while blue states tend to pay more money to the federal government than they receive. I have never been able to convince any conservative person that this is true.

They insist, with zero evidence because none exists, that conservatives are the hard-working people keeping this country going, while the libs just want to give away tax money to lazy people who refuse to work. This is such a core belief for some folks that no amount of evidence can ever convince them of the truth.

Even their own lived experience cannot sway their opinion about this. After all, even if they themselves receive welfare, their core belief tells them welfare is bad. Even if they work like dogs, they continue to believe that poor people are lazy. Even if they never manage to get ahead, they continue to believe in the American dream. The problem, they must secretly believe in their heart of hearts, is them.

Thus their anger.

If you are impervious both to facts and to your own lived experience, I know of no way to change your mind.

Sources:

Moneygeek
The States That Are Most Reliant on Federal Aid
https://www.moneygeek.com/living/states-most-reliant-federal-government/

WHAT CAPITALISTS GET WRONG ABOUT HUMAN MOTIVATION

If money were the only thing, we'd all be in a small list of careers

Making money is only one purpose of work. It's not even the most important purpose. People have always worked, even before we dreamed up the concept of money.

The thing capitalists get completely wrong is their assumption that everyone is motivated by money. It makes sense, of course — that's what motivates them. So if money is the grand motivator for everyone, why don't we all work in finance?

Why do we have preschool teachers, social workers, artists, clergy and cooks?

Why do we have stay-at-home mothers and fathers who are literally on duty day and night in return for no money at all? If you believe people are only motivated by money, it makes sense to have few or no social safety nets.

There are many people who believe everyone is intrinsically lazy and will not lift a finger unless they're handed a buck. Some of these people truly believe it's necessary to threaten the masses with starvation to motivate them to work.

That's why such people shudder at the thought of social safety nets. Why do you think liberals still fight for things like paid parental leave? The U.S. still doesn't have that because the far-right is convinced that some woman somewhere is going to have a baby just to get a few weeks off work. (I have to wonder: Have any of these people given birth? Or cared for a newborn?)

Some leaders are still upset that food stamps exist

From former President Ronald Reagan on, some conservatives have fervently believed that anyone who requires help feeding themselves is just a grifter, out to take somebody else's hard-earned money and probably blow it on steak, lobsters and caviar. That's if they didn't figure out a way to get the cash off the card and use it to buy drugs.

And they're right about some people. Lazy people do exist! Yes, there are some people who, if allowed to do so, will loll around playing video games or fishing all day. Some will take advantage of whatever safety nets we offer.

My son had the best comeback to this I've ever heard. He said he's worked with a few people who didn't have any work ethic at all.

"Let those people stay home," he said. *"I don't want to work with them. They don't add anything to the workplace. They're just in the way."*

I can already hear the critics

"So you're just fine with people sitting on their butts and letting all of us hard-working Americans support them? I have worked 16 hours a day, six days a week, since I was 14. In my spare time, I started two side hustles, both of which turned into multi-million companies before I sold them. Now you want to give my hard-earned money to people like the good-for-nothing nephew my sister coddled all his life, who gets high every day and is always hitting his mom up for cigarette money?"

I will never be able to convince people like that of the truth: Most of us have already been working plenty hard but have not been adequately compensated for it. I would love to live in a society in which talent, hard work and a willingness to accept responsibility always pay off. If young people are losing their faith in capitalism, it's for very good reasons.

The working poor are society's biggest philanthropists

The working poor (unwillingly) donate lavishly to the very rich. That idea blew my mind when I first read it on the last page of the book *Nickel and Dimed: On (Not) Getting By in America*, by the much-missed genius Barbara Ehrenreich. She put into words exactly what I had always felt.

A big chunk of the wealth of the top 1 percent comes directly from failing to adequately compensate the people who work for them. The modern-day robber barons (like their 19th century forebears) did not become rich from their brilliant ideas, hard work, talent, vision or anything else. They may well have all those things, but their real special sauce was being in the right place at the right time, having seed money and contacts — and being willing to squeeze the hell out of their workers.

Most people only think they don't want to work

If they're unemployed, they might appreciate the break for a week or two. But then they start looking for things to do.

They might paint their living room or finally do that landscaping project they never had time to tackle. Maybe they'll start some kind of passion project they always wanted to do. For the most part, people like to work. They enjoy the feeling of accomplishment. Very few people truly want to do nothing. And some of those people who appear to be lazy just need mental health care, another thing we're quite stingy with.

I care about my work. I'm proud of my writing, even though it's never earned me very much money. I bet you care about the things you do, too.

Plenty of good, worthwhile work doesn't pay

If you're a nursing home aid, to give one example, you're severely underpaid, yet you're doing extremely important work you should take pride in. If you do volunteer work, you're serving society without any pay whatsoever.

Why should anyone feel shame for being poor? Your value as a human being has nothing to do with your financial net worth. Are you doing some good in the world, whether it's paid or unpaid?

Maybe you have a black belt in karate and teach karate classes to kids in the evenings. Or you are known for your apple pies and bring them to every charity bake sale. Perhaps every year you help organize your town's biggest festival, play in a pretty good local band on the weekends or do woodworking in your garage. Maybe you're busy raising young children.

There are many, many ways to have a good life. I fervently hope you can earn enough to pay your basic living expenses and that after that you're able to find some time and energy to build a satisfying life that doesn't depend on the system, because for many of us, the system is broken.

Sources:

Barbara Ehrenreich
Nickel and Dimed: On (Not) Getting by in America
https://www.amazon.com/Nickel-Dimed-Not-Getting-America/dp/0312626681

BOOMERS: WORKED. GEN X: IRKED. MILLENNIALS: SHIRKED.

I can't wait to see what Generation Alpha does!

My dad worked for the same company almost my whole life until he retired. Yes, he was actually able to retire — even though he was always an hourly blue-collar employee — because he is a Boomer.

It wasn't a bad deal. He worked his ass off, the company paid him for every hour he was there, and he was eventually able to retire. True, there was a highly contentious 1976 strike that I will never forget, but for the most part both sides got what they needed from each other.

I'm an older Gen X (I missed Boomerhood by just a few years) and I got the message: You need to work your ass off and show some loyalty, but you will be rewarded for it.

I got the wrong message

I worked my ass off and didn't protect my personal time at all. But the work ethic of the younger generation is markedly different from what I've seen.

Good for them, I say.

Boomers would do anything for their work, and we Gen X people followed their examples. We thought we'd also be appreciated, but we were not. Many people in my generation know what it's like to perform thousands of hours of unpaid work and then to be kicked to the curb anyway.

We feel betrayed when this happens: *"I cut my vacation short for you! I took calls when I was hosting guests for you! I performed work while on vacation in another country for you! I missed time with my kids for you! What do you mean, you're done with me now?"*

Yeah. I didn't say anything like that when I was laid off from my newspaper job in 2015, but I sure thought it. I felt as stung and betrayed as if I had been cheated on by a lover whom I'd been supporting for decades.

Because that's the thing: A lot of people my age went all-in on our work. I could tell so many stories. When I visited my now-husband in the Netherlands, I still wrote and emailed in a weekly column. I got a kick out of writing one of them the day "after" it ran, thanks to the magic of the time difference, and wrote about that.

If big news happened on a day I was off, I dropped everything and got my ass right to the newsroom. I took work calls at all hours of the day and night. There was a double murder-suicide on a weekend once, and my staff had already put in 40 hours and I didn't have an overtime budget to pay them more. Off I went to cover it myself. I brought along my unpaid husband as the photographer.

I roped in my husband a lot. He photographed the EF-4 tornado that hit us a decade ago when my photographer was in Chicago and unable to return in time to do it. He did it for free.

He helped me put together the janky old newsroom desks in our new location after the company sold the historic building we'd occupied for 100 years. Yes, the company expected me to reassemble all the desks. They were ancient and falling apart and no two were alike. They were missing parts. It was a lot of work.

It took us all weekend. We did it for free.

Often, the internet at work went down

It was always a scramble.

My home internet served as our backup. One especially stressful night, the internet went down just as we were starting our nightly production, and it stayed down. Of course, not meeting our deadline was not an option, even though we had not been provided with reliable internet.

I disconnected my laptop, ran to my nearby house, and used my home internet to download AP stories, obituaries, the weather forecast info, etc. Then I rushed back to work, reconnected to our system and distributed all the information to everyone who needed it.

Then they'd tell me what else they needed as far as sports stories or whatever, and I'd do another run. It was exhausting and I felt irritated that my own personal internet was our backup system. But by God, we got the paper out on time.

At one point, the company decided to change our computer system, switch the programs we used and fire the editor all at the same time. For a couple of weeks, I corralled all the chaos as city editor before being named as editor. It was a lot.

Once I worked from 5 a.m. one day until 3 a.m. the next day, straight through. I was barely able to find time to use the restroom in that stretch. It was hard. Everything got done, and I'm really proud that it did, but it only happened because I made it happen.

We worked through a blizzard so bad that after we finished, the last page designer and I — I'd sent everyone else home — had to struggle on foot through drifts so deep we could barely get through them. No vehicle short of a snow plow could have gotten through the streets. The drifts were past my waist!

Panting and sweating but also freezing, we managed to make our way to my house, where I cooked midnight spaghetti for us. She had to sleep at my place.

Almost nobody actually saw that paper, but we had to officially publish it or we'd have to refund all the advertising, which would have meant losing thousands of dollars. The company expressed zero appreciation.

The newspaper industry was imploding thanks to the internet destroying its business model, so my experience was no doubt more extreme than that of workers in most other fields. Still, all of us working there gave it our all, trying to keep the inevitable from happening. And we did damned good work under impossible circumstances.

Under my leadership, the paper was recognized for excellence by our state press association every year. One would think all this would count for something. But it didn't.

Of course it didn't. And many people my age can tell similar tales.

The next generation learned important lessons

Just as my generation learned our work ethic by watching our parents, the next generation learned caution from watching mine.

Here's what it boils down to: *"My parents missed a lot of time with me when I was growing up because work was always encroaching on family time. And then they lost their jobs anyway. Yeah, I'm not falling for that bullshit."*

Good. For. Them.

It's not really "shirking" when you're providing the appropriate amount of work for your pay.

Nobody was happier than me when, post-pandemic, corporations had to start courting employees and paying them more. (They didn't court older workers, of course. I eventually gave up on getting hired and went all-in on freelance.) I laugh my ass off when I drive by the sign announcing my local Taco Bell is paying $15 per hour.

That's awesome! Those people at Taco Bell are making more than my reporters or paginators or photographers did. Because I worked so much unpaid overtime, they are making more than I made as editor of a daily paper — and when they leave work, they don't have to worry about it again until the next time they clock in.

I worked in fast food as a student so I know these jobs can

be harder and more stressful than people give fast food workers credit for. But one thing I can say about it is when you are off work, it's out of your head. Unless you're in management, you're not taking emergency work calls at home. *"The napkin dispenser is empty and nobody here knows where the napkins are kept! You gotta come in and save us!"*

Nope.

For a couple of years, I worked another job, mostly with millennials. I quickly learned it was not safe to get between them and the door at 5 p.m. because they'd trample you. I had no problem working past 5 p.m. if I were in the middle of something, but I was definitely the only one there who felt that way.

Initially, I thought badly of them for it. But they were right and I was wrong. It made absolutely no sense for them to donate extra time like that.

It really irks me that I gave so much of myself away.

I'm irked that I didn't take all my vacation time because they didn't provide enough workers to cover me.

I'm irked that I had to hit up my husband to help me sometimes.

I'm irked that once, when my son was a young teen, I called him and told him there were various leftovers for his dinner but I'd have to work late again. My daughter was at college and my husband was working a late shift at that point, so my son was on his own. And then I called him later and asked him what he'd eaten, and he answered, *"A can of frosting."*

At that point, I left work and cooked the kid a real dinner, which I served around 9 p.m. That was bullshit!

Employers can't have it both ways. Either employees are valued and will reap the rewards of all their work and sacrifice, or they'll face employees who feel zero loyalty and won't do anything more than the duties they are explicitly paid to perform.

My generation of chumps was screwed, and I'm still plenty irked. And bitter. Generation Alpha, I hope you're paying attention.

A GLUT OF ELITES? NO, IT'S MUCH WORSE THAN THAT

*Capitalism has a glut of
ordinary humans now*

There's a theory that our colleges have overproduced elites. But it's not just the elites we have a glut of.

I'm no elite

I do not have a graduate degree. I earned a bachelor's degree from a state school. But I think I speak for millions of resentful unemployed or underemployed people who wrongly thought they'd earned the right to a reasonably enjoyable career that would cover the costs of a basic middle-class life. That's what we were promised.

For millions of us, the world either doesn't value our skills, values them but lacks a sustainable business model to pay for them or only needs a small number of us to fill the few available jobs. We have to figure out some other way to live. Naturally, we're unhappy about this.

I got a journalism degree and spent 30 years in community journalism, finishing up as editor of a small-town daily newspaper. That it did not pay well and required enormous amounts of unpaid labor to do it right didn't change the fact that it fulfilled me and provided a steady paycheck that (barely) covered the cost of my ultra-thrifty lifestyle. I'm still not over my job disappearing.

I will never be over it

The work of telling people what is going on in the community is crying out to be done, and many of us very much want to do this work, but we can't. Many shenanigans are occurring outside the public view. I hear about a few of them and know the staff I used to lead would have an absolute field day covering these stories. People ask me all the time why I don't just cover them myself, and the answer is that covering the news is not a hobby.

It takes significant work and brings in very little money. Who is going to pay me to sit at a council meeting, sift through courthouse filings, interview school board members, show up at a murder scene?

Couldn't I collect advertising to pay my expenses? That's yet another full-time job and one for which I am unsuited.

I still have lots of journalism contacts and I know about an awful lot of talented journalists who are trying to do this kind of thing, and most of them can't make it work. I know of one man who used to teach at one of the top journalism schools who now runs a weekly newspaper – at a loss. He works another job and uses his salary to support himself and his newspaper.

You may know a brilliant barista

It's no wonder more young people are skipping college, understanding that it's no longer a certain way to a comfortable living but that it is a certain way to immense debt. It took about a generation for people to realize that the risks and benefits of a college degree had turned upside down. The barista at your favorite coffee shop may well have more education than most of her customers.

It's true that we don't have a lot of job openings for history or philosophy professors. Or for literature majors. Or, sadly, for journalists. Since my degree was in journalism, with an English minor, I of course deserve my fate.

But we only need so many engineers and lawyers. For that matter, if every young person becomes a plumber – the job conservatives seem to believe should be the ambition of every teenager – the plumbers will soon be in hot water, too.

We don't just have a glut of elites who are angry they cannot land cushy elite jobs. We have a lot of non-elites who are angry they cannot even land OK-ish jobs. The Nobody Wants To Work Anymore brigade is talking about unskilled jobs without benefits, like cashiers and servers, that can't support a family. The NWTWA people are just mad that they have to wait longer for a table and when they're finally seated, their server is too overstretched to wait on them hand and foot.

Middle-class jobs are scarce, no matter what any pundit claims. Talk to real people with education, skills and experience who are trying to find jobs a notch or two above entry-level, and you will hear tales of frustration, anger, fear and defeat.

Work and jobs are not the same thing

Meanwhile, we have a lot of important work going undone because we can't figure out how to pay for it.

Journalism is the obvious example, and I use it because it's the world I understand. We desperately need professional, well-trained people to perform actual journalism – not public relations, not propaganda, not sales copy pretending to be news – but actual journalism. I have known hundreds of newspaper journalists through the years. Most of them were dedicated people who did their best, especially at the community level where I was content to serve.

If you want to know what happens when nobody is actually covering your news anymore, look around and see who is in office.

The same is true in many other fields. Have you tried to place an elderly loved one in a nursing home? You will pay $10K per month and the place will be so understaffed that your loved one may not be fed, bathed or toileted appropriately.

The horror of sitting in a full, leaking diaper of your own waste, desperately hungry and thirsty but unable to obtain nourishment, is a fate many of us will face someday because we refuse to hire, pay and value enough caregivers.

Nobody wants to perform childcare because the business model doesn't work – the cost of providing daycare exceeds what most parents can afford to pay. Yet even parents who yearn to stay home with their baby for a few years often can't afford to take time out. The work is important but the very people who may be the most motivated to do it well (the baby's parents) can't afford to.

After the agricultural revolution and until the last 150 years or so, most humans spent most of their time farming and preparing food, but few of us are farmers now and plenty of people don't even cook. At most, they might combine a can of this and a box of that and call it "cooking."

This is because we have arranged modern life so that nobody values housekeeping, childcare and food preparation. People who perform these tasks suffer from lack of status, even though the things they do are desperately needed. They are far more important than, say, the work of a hedge fund manager or a digital advertising specialist.

We can eat and clothe ourselves with relative ease. We have enough housing for all, too – although not all of it is where the demand is, and too much of it sits empty as investment properties.

So the question arises: What good are humans, anyway? What are any of them good for? We don't just have a glut of postdocs. We have a glut of everyone, and AI is making more of us redundant every week.

This is where we are now:

We don't need people to do much of anything that's important. AI and tech handle a good proportion of what people used to spend their days doing for pay.

Other things that are very important but for which we have no viable business model (journalism, elder care, child care) are poorly done if done at all.

People still need to work because all this abundance modern technology provides costs a lot of money, and we would rather let you die than let you have what you need without paying for it.

Do we have to monetize everything?

Why can't we champion learning and education without tying it to paid careers? Do we really think we should drop the torch of literature, philosophy and history? Does absolutely everything have to be monetized?

I don't think the answer is to stop encouraging education in favor of the trades. I think we need more education, not less. A classical education is for everyone, even if they never earn a dime from it. Even for plumbers, mechanics and other people who work in the trades.

I read a lot, and not just novels and news. I have not formally studied anthropology or sociology beyond a few electives, but I read books on these subjects because I want to. How did I know I wanted to learn more about these subjects? It's because I got a taste from those college electives, and my best teachers taught me how to continue learning on my own.

That's why I shake my head when people say you only need to take classes in your major, as if the only purpose of education is to learn how to make money.

Most people may as well be illiterate

They know how to read and write, but it does them little good because they don't know how to think. They never read anything longer than a tweet and they don't understand how to evaluate a news source. This is the tl;dr generation.

Mention something from history and they may know nothing about it. But this will not stop them from having strong opinions based on some 280-word post they once read while sitting on the toilet.

I was talking to a woman (over the phone) with much more formal education than I have one day during the Covid lockdowns. She felt these lockdowns were intolerable. I said people in our time had gotten off pretty lucky, historically speaking, and mentioned the London Blitz as an example of a time when ordinary people suffered much worse. She didn't know what I was talking about.

No wonder she questioned Covid restrictions. From her perspective, her suffering was just about at the max of what any human should be expected to deal with. A bit of history would have done her some good.

Whether you're a history postdoc or a laid-off journalist with only a bachelor's degree, your education is not wasted. The world might make you take a job doing something you didn't exactly dream of, but the point of education was never to make money or gain status. If you don't know that, maybe your education *was* wasted on you.

WHY ARE THE POOR STILL WITH US?

Apparently, we like our system this way

There is no reason for anybody to be poor anymore.

This is especially true in places like the U.S. We have more than enough resources for everyone. The problem isn't that we can't produce enough. The problem is greed.

Some people struggle to find interesting new ways to waste money while others struggle to meet their basic needs.

We have more than enough housing
Much of it sits empty while families live on the street.

We have more than enough food
We throw away 40 percent of it, even as some people search through dumpsters to find something to eat.

We have plenty of resources for healthcare
We spend the most and get the least of all industrialized countries because we utterly refuse to fix our convoluted system. Since it benefits the powerful, the rest of us must suffer.

We could cut our national healthcare costs by $450 billion per year if we adopted a single-payer system, according to the Yale School of Public Health. (That's enough to cover everyonet's college with plenty left over!)

So what's the problem? We are living in a land of milk and honey no one in history could have dreamed of, and I bet I know what you are thinking right now: Even the richest person in the world 100 years ago would have envied the things available to a working-class American today.

And it's true
Money could not buy the advantages we have now.

We can stay cool in the summer and warm in the winter with the turn of a dial. We women, we can (for now, at least) avoid endless childbearing.

If we do have a family, most of us will never have to endure the agony of burying multiple children. We don't die from minor infections. We can eat fresh fruits and vegetables in the dead of winter. We can still see and hear in our old age. We can travel long distances without the hardships of yesteryear.

It's a freaking paradise!

Except it's not
Income inequality is one of the great evils of our time because it is wasteful — of everything.

The waste of housing and food are bad enough, but we are wasting human lives, too. Nobody will ever know how many geniuses spend their lives doing mundane things because we didn't give them any opportunities.

The system works great for those in power. The people in power have zero incentive to change the system, and the people with no power have zero ability to change the system.

Once you start looking for examples of income inequality, you will see them everywhere
And you will wonder why we've chosen to pay some people so little and others so much. There's a polite fiction we pretend to believe that says the hardest workers will be rewarded and the poor are just a bunch of slackers, but we all know that's untrue.

If you don't know that's untrue, shame on you. You are willfully choosing not to see it. And that probably means you're benefiting

We need a new academic discipline to focus on income inequality

Much as Critical Race Theory helps expose the way racism is woven into our society to benefit some at the expense of others, we need to expose the ways that income inequality is also a feature, not a bug, in our system. So is sexism.

I think rigorous academic study would show that many times, all these threads are entwined into a tangle of injustice.

Sources:

The United Way of the National Capital Area
Vacant Homes vs. Homelessness in Cities Around the U.S.
https://unitedwaynca.org/blog/vacant-homes-vs-homelessness-by-city/#:~:text=Sixteen%20million%20homes%20currently%20sit,thousands%20of%20Americans%20face%20homelessness.

Feeding America
Fighting food waste and hunger through food rescue
https://www.feedingamerica.org/our-work/reduce-food-waste#:~:text=Each%20year%2C%20119%20billion%20pounds,food%20in%20America%20is%20wasted.

The Commonwealth Fund
Mirror, Mirror 2021: Reflecting Poorly
Health Care in the U.S. Compared to Other High-Income Countries
https://www.commonwealthfund.org/publications/fund-reports/2021/aug/mirror-mirror-2021-reflecting-poorly?gad=1&gclid=CjwKCAjwge2iBhBBEiwAfXDBRx8rAnd3GXqd6rQzDDwtiLf1SzK9ZM-Siuo4dTNk6kNF0RYsPplvfBoCmTkQAvD_BwE

Yale School of Public Health
Study: More Than 335,000 Lives Could Have Been Saved During

Pandemic if U.S. Had Universal Health Care
https://ysph.yale.edu/news-article/yale-study-more-than-335000-lives-could-have-been-saved-during-pandemic-if-us-had-universal-health-care/#:~:text=%E2%80%9CA%20single%2Dpayer%20health%20care,per%20year%2C%E2%80%9D%20Galvani%20said.

WHY 'DON'T SPEND MONEY YOU DON'T HAVE' IS DUMB ADVICE

It's something only privileged people say

Most financial advice is dumb.

Occasionally some of it is helpful. But plenty of it is harmful, and *"Don't spend money you don't have"* is the worst. So is *"never use a credit card."*

- Yes, I know I'm spurting blood. It's fine. I'm saving up until I can afford to get stitches.
- There's no heat in the house, and the baby is crying, but I'm not getting the furnace repaired until I can hand over cash for it. If the baby is so darned concerned about the subzero temps, she can pay for the furnace herself.
- I'm broke and payday isn't for three more days. So yeah, I'm hungry, but I'm not going into debt for a loaf of bread and a jar of peanut butter.
- I didn't budget for a tree branch to land on my roof. Sucks that rain is pouring into my living room, but I'm saving up. If I get some overtime this week, I'll probably have enough for a tarp by the weekend.

Sometimes, you need to spend money whether you have it or not

I've never in my life been short on money because I blew more than I could afford on a stupid luxury. *Never.*

It's always been something like a medical cost or a home or car repair. These things are unpredictable. Ideally, you would be able to pay for them with your emergency fund, but an emergency fund itself is a luxury not everyone can afford.

Neither is a budget. You may not have enough money to put adequate funds into every category. If you have enough money to budget $400 per month for entertainment, for example, you can stick to that. If you do not have enough money to budget anything for entertainment, you will still, inevitably, spend at least a few bucks on some form of entertainment occasionally. You are human and you deserve to see a movie or go out to eat a couple times a year.

If you're poor, your best bet is to take an honest look at your income and expenses, cut your costs the best you can and hang on for dear life while looking for any opportunity to increase your income.

You prioritize your rent/mortgage, utilities, transportation, healthcare and groceries. You cut these as much as you possibly can, and you recognize that sometimes devastating things happen and you will have no choice but to pay up.

Sometimes, going into debt makes sense

When you're young, you have all the expenses of forming a household and, usually, the lowest pay of your life.

But you need to live somewhere, and in most cases, you need a car to get to work. If you want to make more than entry-level pay, you're probably going to need some kind of education or job training. There are at least four good reasons to spend money you don't have:
- Buying a house, usually
- Buying a car, sometimes
- Paying for college, usually
- Obtaining a necessity such as food or medical care, always

What if your refrigerator quits?

You can bet your ass I did not have a line item in my (mental) budget for a new refrigerator. The old one was only around six years old and should have been fine for many more years. But it would be ridiculous to say you shouldn't purchase a new refrigerator until you have the cash saved up.

What if your car conks out? This is a big one. Trying to keep reliable transportation is a killer for those of us who don't live in an urban area with reliable public transportation. It's virtually impossible to do without a car in much of the U.S.

If you can swing a car payment, you can drive a more reliable car, but if you try to save money by keeping a beater, there are going to be times when it isn't running. If you can do some of your own repairs, great, but you probably will need to pay to have the old car towed to a garage and fixed when the repairs are too extensive.

I once heard someone (with money) state *"People always have enough money for the things that are important to them."*

She didn't know how deep that remark cut. I did not in fact have enough money for the things that were important to me at that point, and it was not because I was blowing any money.

Discretionary income is a lovely thing

Those who have it and have always had it tend not to be able to comprehend that there are millions of people — including those who work full time — who don't make enough money to pay all their expenses with enough left to save and invest.

People who make a certain amount of money honestly think that full-time workers just need to make better budgeting decisions. *"Stop having your nails done or buying fancy coffee or taking yearly vacations or owning a big-screen TV!"*

If only I had a dollar for each time I've heard a better-off person advise somebody like me to save money by dropping luxuries I already never spent money on!

Save up an emergency fund as soon as you can

It took me years and years and years to save up enough money to allow me to smooth out all the big and little emergencies that come up. Once I finally did, I prioritized keeping that money set aside.

It would be easy to justify tapping my emergency fund for any number of other things. But that emergency fund has saved our ass so many times. When I was a new young homeowner, I once had no choice but to blow money on a high-interest-rate loan in order to replace a furnace.

Now? When my husband was on workers comp after breaking his leg in an industrial accident, having that money saved us.

I felt very, very grateful to have that emergency fund then.

An occasional latte or piece of avocado toast is not the problem

In general, these excuses make handy heuristics so that people who have a comfortable standard of living will always have a way to explain to themselves why other people aren't as well-off as they are.

It's so, so nice to blame others' financial positions on what you assume to be their terrible choices. *"She's carrying a nice purse! That's why she's poor!"*

Yeah. It's her purse (a gift or a knock-off for all we know) that's the problem here. It's not our society at all. It's certainly not the fact that the middle class has become an endangered species.

According to the U.S. Bureau of Labor Statistics, the median hourly wage is $23.11. The person making that pay could easily spend half of it on rent, depending on where they live. Such a person essentially has no discretionary income.

I understand this very well. Never in my life, including when I was the editor of a daily newspaper or a copywriter for an ad agency, did I manage to make the median wage. Only the fact that I live in an area with a low cost of living allowed me to survive.

Better financial advice for the working poor exists

But you won't often hear it from people with plenty of money. They aren't living on the same planet as the working class, so their advice, even when kindly meant, often doesn't apply.

I do believe in living a simple lifestyle. I've never paid to have my nails done in my life, and I make my coffee at home. I take it a lot further than that, actually – I hang my laundry up to dry and make my own bread! – but not everyone is going to make the same choices.

I have some better advice

First of all: Be aware of every penny coming into and leaving your house.

You can't make good financial decisions until you thoroughly understand where all your money is coming from and where all of it is going.

Once you know exactly what you're paying for everything, you can make the right choices for you.

For years, I wrote everything down on a piece of notebook paper. Now I check online.

You control money for that short period of time it's in your control, and not every decision you make is going to be a decision you want to make. Many times, you'll be forced to spend money in a way you do not want and did not plan ... like expensive medical bills. Or a new refrigerator.

Get over it. That's how life is.

I use a credit card for virtually everything

Yes, I know, lots of experts say to do the opposite. Ignore them. Those experts are too rich to know how money works for the non-wealthy. If they had been limited to the income I've had in my lifetime, they'd change their tune.

No, I don't assume my credit card is magic and that I can use it to buy anything that strikes my fancy. (If you struggle with that, this method is not for you.)

My credit card is real money and I'm aware that it's not free. But it's safer to carry a card than a big wad of cash, and the one time I had a fraudulent charge, it took a single phone call to remove it. If your cash is stolen, you're out of luck. Your debit card has limited protection compared to your credit card. Mine appears pristine and unused.

I arranged to have the balance on my credit card paid off automatically every month. In my single-mom years, I couldn't do that, but I got back to it as soon as I could.

Why do I use my credit card?
It makes me nervous to carry a lot of cash.

By using my credit card, I can take advantage of a really good deal without stopping to count the money in my wallet or hitting an ATM first. If black beans (a staple for us) are marked down at the store, I can stock up on a case of them. If the past-their-prime bananas are going cheap, I buy lots of them, then I bake and freeze massive quantities of banana bread. If there's a big-ticket item I've been planning to purchase (say, a lawn mower) and I happen to run into a deal, I can snap it up.

This also gives me a very favorable credit score, which is good to have for lots of reasons. You can also earn cash-back or frequent flier miles.

Also? If you want to see exactly where your money went, you can see every credit card purchase online. Cash just evaporates without leaving a trace unless you keep every receipt or write everything down.

Decide whether you really want to keep up with the Joneses
I decided to let the Jones family win.

I do not care one bit whether my jeans are in style. Did the waistline or hem move up or down this season? I don't care. I own a pair of jeans and I will wear them until they're worn out.

My house follows zero fashions. It is unique and custom because we did so much of the work ourselves. We furnished it in an eclectic manner as we went along. Nobody else has to like it, but we love it.

My dogs are mutts from a shelter. I will never pay hundreds of dollars for purebred dogs when the shelters are full of sweet, loving pets who need a home.

We own two cars. Both are ancient. We don't have any friends who make judgments based on what cars people drive.

Ignore the world of advertising

Everybody is trying to sell you something, but you can decide not to play. Don't purchase anything you don't need. When something wears out and you need to replace it, make a thoughtful choice without being swayed by ads.

I've written advertising for a living before. Trust me, you can safely ignore it.

Our society isn't fair

We do not live in a meritocracy. Talent and hard work aren't always rewarded. You can get mad all you want, and should. Our system should change in profound ways.

But also? Stop expecting the people whose money comes pouring out of a spigot to understand how money (mostly) fails to trickle down.

Shit happens and will always happen

That could have been the title of this book.

Sometimes you will have enough money to cover it. Sometimes you will not — even if you're trying very hard.

You can make very good decisions and still be screwed.

Some people are poor because they made unfortunate choices. Some never finished high school, had children before they were ready for them, indulged themselves with expensive lifestyles, etc.

Those people are in the minority, but there's a pervasive myth that every struggling person is in that position because of bad decisions, not because our system has failed us.

One of the most hurtful lies fed to Americans is that if we do all the right things, we will live good lives

Those of us who got good grades, earned a college degree, worked hard, accepted responsibility at our jobs, put off having children until we married and established a career, lived a simple lifestyle and tried hard to save money yet still find ourselves struggling know this is untrue. People with chronic health problems (or with a disabled spouse or child) will face even greater challenges.

The system has worked fine for many people, but it's failed close to half of us. The people who have thrived in this system congratulate themselves for their success. This allows some of them to avoid caring very much about how others are struggling. Hey, we all had exactly the same chances and opportunities, but the rich were obviously smarter and harder-working than the rest of us, we are told.

Most people are embarrassed to be making a low or modest income

We blame ourselves. We seldom understand that if about half the country is struggling, it's not us; it's the system.

That keeps us from demanding the system change. We look up from our hamster wheels and see that we're not getting anywhere, and then we try to run a little faster. If we just try harder, we think, we will finally get where we need to be.

Good luck with that.

Sources:

U.S. Bureau of Labor Statistics
May 2023 National Occupational Employment and Wage Estimates
https://www.bls.gov/oes/current/oes_nat.htm

MY OLD CAST IRON SKILLET EXPLAINS A LOT

*Why do we mindlessly ignore
our own best interests?*

I have two cast iron skillets that used to be my mother's, and actually, I believe one of them was my grandmother's. It's hard to say, because I've had them forever.

I admit I didn't always use my cast iron hand-me-downs, for the same reason they ended up in my hands in the first place: I thought I needed fancy non-stick pans, when all I really needed was a five-minute lesson on how to cook with cast iron.

I promise you, a properly seasoned cast iron skillet allows you to make things like over-easy eggs or an omelet (or pizza!) without sticking a bit.

The surface is just as slick and stick-free as a brand-new nonstick pan. Plus, these skillets are easy to care for. The one downside is their weight; if you have back or wrist problems, they might be too difficult to lift.

They are inexpensive and will last for generations

Buy one for $20 (even less from a thrift store) and you're done. You never have to buy another one, ever. Your great-grandkids will use it after you're gone, if you've taught them how. That's good news for you but bad news for Big Skillet. How much money is there in skillets if each family buys one or two every 50 years?

So naturally, marketers do everything they can to convince us to pay more for non-stick skillets that will wear out every few years.

We are so easily suckered

We make decisions all the time for reasons that, if we stop to think, make little sense. (Maybe that's why we're kept busy scrolling — so we don't stop to think very much.)

Why do we keep buying expensive cookware that we have to replace every few years when we could use the same pan all our lives and then pass it on to several generations?

As soon as you start thinking about this, you realize your choice of cookware is just one of a thousand examples of mindless waste and bad decisions that don't benefit us but do benefit some corporation.

I've started asking a simple question.

Does this choice benefit me, or some corporation? It's amazing how often it's the latter.

Did paying any attention to fashion do me any good?

Admittedly, I didn't pay much attention in the first place, but I ignore fashion now even more. I wear the same basic clothing year after year, only replacing things when they actually wear out.

That's more money in my pocket, less waste and less environmental degradation.

What about keeping up with home decor trends?

I couldn't do this even if I wanted to, and it forced me to follow my eclectic inclinations. My house is full of things I've picked up off the street (a cool old church bench that's now in my parlor!) or purchased second-hand (the antique dining room set I love) or was given to me by someone who knew I'd appreciate it (an indescribable marble-topped wooden side table with a curved door). Everything is quirky and timeless and I love it so much.

What do I want to eat?

Nothing from a chain. I've never had Chipotle or Popeyes or Five

Guys or Texas Roadhouse, etc. I'd much rather eat my own cooking than something consultants have fine-tuned to appeal to a certain demographic.

I'm sure those places have food that tastes just fine. Some of it is probably really good. But when I eat out, give me a unique restaurant that someone opened out of passion. Any place where the owner's family makes up most of the staff and the older ones still speak with a heavy accent is usually a good bet.

How did I want to feed my babies?

Because I was lucky and because I made it a point to educate myself and prepare very well, I was able to breastfeed exclusively. Formula was pushed relentlessly in those days (I gave birth in 1989 and 1992) by some of the best marketers the world has ever known. For example, a free case of ready-to-feed formula showed up at my house right at the two-week growth spurt, exactly when their marketers knew quite well that many mothers waver in their confidence to nurse. Pissed, I directed the UPS delivery guy to return it. Some parents are unable to nurse, of course, and in those cases, formula fills a need.

How do I clean my house?

I use vinegar and baking soda a lot. You don't need most prepared cleaning products. They're more expensive and often less effective.

How do I dry my clothes?

On a clothesline. Or on indoor racks during bad weather. It's just my husband and me now, but we also did this when the kids were living at home. (In winter, I like hanging up a rack of wet laundry right in my bedroom just before bed. It's my free humidifier!) It costs nothing to hang up your clothes, and it's less damaging to the fabric so everything holds up better. Why spend money on something that happens naturally for free?

What kind of pets do I adopt?

I love my rescue mutts. Why spend hundreds on a purebred

when there are sweet dogs and cats being euthanized every day? I can't bear to think about that. Save a dog or cat instead.

What automobiles do I drive?

You don't need an SUV or a minivan or a truck unless you have a large family or are a contractor or farmer, etc. I had two car seats in the back of an old Chevette when all the other moms had minivans. It was fine.

Our cars are small and ancient. We won't get rid of them until we have to, even though we're missing out on lots of technology. My cars are unaware cell phones exist, for example. Oh well. Both the Civic and the Mini have manual transmissions, too. The average car payment for new cars is now $729. That's more than most of the house payments I've made in my life! I haven't had a car payment for well over a decade and don't plan to ever have one again.

I think I've made my point. It's not that I'm smarter or more thoughtful than anyone else. But as much as possible, I attempt to make every decision based on what's best for me, for society and for the world, not on somebody's marketing.

You can still live, though

After one of my stories on Medium (*We Could Learn a Lot About Sex From the Dutch*) went viral and brought in more than $20,000, we did indulge in a few small pleasures – a new patio and grill, a small seasonal pool and some other miscellaneous things we'd been putting off – but I tucked most of it away for the future.

A good emergency fund is one of the best luxuries and serves as a terrific sleep aid, too.

Sources:

Bankrate
Average car payments in 2024: What to expect
https://www.bankrate.com/loans/auto-loans/average-monthly-car-payment/#:~:text=the%20best%20deal.-,Car%20payment

%20statistics,of%202023%20were%20used%20vehicles.

Medium

We Could Learn a Lot About Sex From the Dutch
https://medium.com/minds-without-borders/we-could-learn-a-lot-about-sex-from-the-dutch-8864066b2d99

THIS ONE IS FOR ALL THE WELL-EDUCATED, CULTURED, HARD-WORKING POOR PEOPLE

… and anyone who thinks we live in a meritocracy

This note from a reader made me laugh:

I always just kind of assumed that you were a bit of a bohemian and secretly posh behind all that. You could have easily fooled me.

In fact you still do. I can't quite buy into the image of you as a genuine impoverished person. You seem much too well-educated and cultured to pull off being poor.

I am not saying this to be rude or anything, just observing the difference between your image and your self-described financial situation.

I don't blame that person all — in fact, I'm grateful for her comment. It gives me an excuse to talk about something I believe is very important:

Many people believe we live in a meritocracy, but we do not.
At all.

I don't know why anybody believes in meritocracy

It's a core belief in America: If you're a smart person who gets an education and works hard, you'll do well.

That's not true, and it's a harmful belief. For one thing, if you honestly believe the American Dream is open to anyone willing to work for it, why donate to charity? Poor people are only getting what they have coming, right? They deserve scorn for not being willing to put forth effort, don't they?

I figured out early on that hard work and talent are not enough.

I had an advantage that most people do not: For most of my adult life, I have lived outside the bubble.

Most people lack that experience. They live in bubbles that contain only people just like themselves.

- Most middle-class people live, work and socialize with other middle-class people.
- Most poor people live, work and socialize with other poor people.
- Most wealthy people live, work and socialize with other wealthy people.

Whatever the norms are in your social group, you assume they are the norms for others. Most people never question it.

But in my former career as a journalist, I met all kinds of people from all kinds of bubbles. Homeless people. CEOs. Members of Congress. Main street shop owners. Factory owners. Prison wardens. People who just got out of jail. Artists. Executives.

It didn't take long for me to learn that there are many "successful" people who are not particularly intelligent or hard-working — and that there are many "unsuccessful" people who are extremely intelligent and hard-working.

To be sure, there are plenty of people for whom hard work, education and intelligence really have paid off — but it's certainly no guarantee and there is always an element of luck involved. Always.

Every single time.

This is important

The U.S. has so many problems and most Americans can't begin to understand what we should be doing to solve them, because we still think that our system fundamentally works.

The foundation of our system is fundamentally messed up, and nothing we try to build on top of it is ever going to work well.

People who know me invariably assume I must have more money than I actually have. Unlike most Americans, I'm not shy about talking about money, because I do not see my income as a reflection of my worth.

On the contrary, I take a lot of pride in having managed to build a good life in spite of never having been paid well. It's taken a lot of creativity and hard work.

If I had a dollar for every person who has said someone with my education, talent and drive ought to be able to land a good job, I wouldn't need a job.

The truth is, there's very little value in being a good writer. Mediocre writers are good enough and are everywhere, and most people in a position to hire a copywriter or content writer are unable to distinguish between a good writer and a poor writer anyway. Not to mention the increasing role of Artificial Intelligence.

The market values some kinds of people with some kinds of skills far beyond others. That's just how it is — it is how it has always been.

You can whine about it — I do — but you can't change it. You can try to get a job doing something that kills your soul, although there's no guarantee you can get such a job.

You can also content yourself with making a low salary and figure out how to make the best of it. That's what I've done.

POVERTY ISN'T WHAT IT USED TO BE

That's why we can't measure it

What does it mean to be poor, anyway?

Economists and governments measure poverty in many different ways, but the best measure is how you feel. People know when they are poor, and they know when they are not.

I know what it is like to be poor, working class and middle class. Each time I shift from one or the other, I feel it — physically. When I've shifted down, I've felt the weight of it. When things have improved, I've felt the burden lift.

You can't define these things. I'm not going to say how many dollars you need to have to qualify as middle class. But when you get there, you know.

The U.S. first set its measurement of poverty by taking the cost of a minimal food diet and multiplying it by three. That may have made sense at the time but it doesn't now because for most of us, buying food is the least of our problems.

Do you have food, clothing and shelter?

These three things are no longer a good measure of well-being in the U.S.

Let me explain.

Food is the least of our problems now.

Except in extraordinary circumstances, no Americans starve to death. There is food, even if it's not great food. In the U.S., there are food pantries that can help you if you don't qualify for food stamps.

And even though groceries are expensive, they are not the top expense for most people. One can still eat a decent diet on a tight budget if you are willing (and able) to cook from scratch.

It may be a different story in the future, though. I don't need to tell you how much grocery prices have risen in recent years.

Clothing isn't even an issue

Most of us have more clothes than we need. Even people who are poor by anyone's measure stuff clothing they don't want into charity boxes. We might not be *Vogue*-ready, but we aren't in danger of exposing our bits from lack of duds.

The idea that poor people are walking around in rags, as they did in the past, is ridiculous. That fashionable woman who just walked by may have purchased her outfit from a thrift shop for just a few dollars.

Yet, some people will shame her for not looking poor enough if she pays for her groceries with what we used to call food stamps.

Now let's talk about shelter

That's the big one. Millions of Americans are priced out of buying houses, and many can't even afford to rent. You have homeless people living in their cars or couch-surfing with family members.

I am thankful to have "cheap" housing where I live. I can't imagine the anxiety of having to come up with a couple of thousand bucks every month just for a place to be.

Even in the cities where housing is most unaffordable, we could, if we wanted, start funding the construction of affordable apartment buildings. We've chosen not to do this.

Forget food, clothing and shelter

We need to change this to food, shelter and healthcare.

Looking at the bills that followed my lumpectomy, I mentioned to my husband how inexpensive a certain doctor I saw as a kid was. At the end of the visit, my parents could just write a check.

Without thinking, I asked him how much a medical visit cost when he was a kid.

"I never paid for a doctor's visit until I came here," he reminded me. That's because he is Dutch, and in the Netherlands, they have the silly idea that everybody should have good medical care.

Apparently, Americans believe if you are poor, you should just die.

There's a reason women are deciding not to have children.

Sure, some women don't want to have kids for any number of reasons, but plenty of others who do want kids can't afford to have them.

The cost of daycare is extreme

A close relative was paying $1,200 per month for one preschool-aged child! This is considerably more than my mortgage payment. Isn't that insane?

I was very hopeful that Biden's Build Back Better plan would pass, as it contained a child tax credit that would have made my relative's life much easier. Sen. Joe Manchin, D-W.Va., killed that, allegedly telling his colleagues he believed parents would just spend the money on drugs.

Why do we accept a system in which one hateful, prejudiced, ill-informed man can hurt millions of people?

I personally think it's a good thing if more people choose not to overwhelm the planet with more children, but I also think that people who want to have kids ought to be able to afford to do so.

Babies should not be a luxury for just the rich.

I was lucky to attend college before it became so expensive

I graduated with zero in student loans. Young people today are seldom that lucky.

This country is full of people under 40 who are smart, hard-working and well-educated and who look like they're doing fine, but who are actually poor as hell. They'll never be able to buy a house or have children because they'll spend most of their prime working years chipping away at their student loans.

We could make college affordable if we wanted to.
We decided not to.

We know how to help poor people

We give them money! Most people use it wisely. Multiple experiments in providing direct payments to the poor have proven that most people don't blow it. Most use it to improve their lives.

Who knows better than the individual what their needs are? Nobody. Some people will spend extra money on food. Others will spend it on childcare or education or a better living situation.

Unfortunately, a lot of people who have always been well-off truly believe that people are poor because they are stupid, lazy or addicted to drugs or alcohol. They believe poor people are unable to make good decisions, because if they made good decisions, they wouldn't be poor.

Yet, a temporary infusion of cash can help poor people improve their situation considerably, such that they eventually no longer need help.

Few people believe this. They will tell you that if you give a poor person money, they'll just stop working. They never worry about whether wealthy people work, though. That's because they hold deep prejudices against poor people.

The truth is, people all over the income spectrum make both good and bad decisions

Is it a smart decision for a rich person to pay $600 for a bottle of wine? Or to purchase a designer handbag instead of one from Target? Come on. I've seen both rich and poor people blow money.

Here's how the rich are different — when they blow some money, nobody judges them for it.

Sources:

U.S. Census

The History of the Official Poverty Measure
https://www.census.gov/topics/income-poverty/poverty/about/history-of-the-poverty-measure.html#:~:text=The%20current%20official%20poverty%20measure,account%20for%20other%20family%20expenses.

Huffpost
Joe Manchin Privately Told Colleagues Parents Use Child Tax Credit Money On Drugs
https://www.huffpost.com/entry/joe-manchin-build-back-better-child-tax-credit-drugs_n_61bf8f6be4b061afe394006d

University of Oxford
The evidence behind putting money directly in the pockets of the poor
https://www.ox.ac.uk/news/science-blog/evidence-behind-putting-money-directly-pockets-poor

HOW DID WE DECIDE SOME ADVANTAGES ARE FAIR GAME AND OTHERS ARE NOT?

We are quite judgy about some of them

Some people are celebrated for taking advantage of the cards they were dealt at birth.

Others are shamed for it.

In sports, talent and training only take you so far.

Having a certain body type can be a big part of your success. Gymnasts and ballerinas are petite. Linebackers are not. Basketball players are tall. Jockeys are short.

We give Olympic medals and sports contracts to people who excel, but we don't talk about how much of it is due to the genetic lottery.

All the training in the world will not make your body suitable for serious mountaineering if you don't have certain genes that help you thrive at high altitudes.

The other side of this is also true

Having the right genes won't do much for you if you don't put in the work.

A successful business career isn't all about talent. We pretend business is a meritocracy, but it isn't.

Still, most people believe they earned their success. I've never met a person who recognized that they succeeded for any reason other than their hard work and skills. They will say they worked hard and that's probably true. They don't realize that others worked just as hard or harder.

People who succeed because of their personality and connections tend to be the ones who most fervently believe in the meritocracy myth.

I think they need to believe this

It would cause a painful rift in their sense of self to admit otherwise.

Every human being is unique. Our bodies, personalities and inborn talents are not exactly like those of anyone else.

And we reward some things but not others.

- Jackson is a fantastic accountant because he happened to be born with an affinity for math. Nobody tells Jackson he shouldn't be using his talents to make money that way.

- Antonia has a wonderful singing voice and practices diligently. It's possible Antonia will become a famous musician, but it's more likely she will sing for a local bar band on the weekends and do something else for a living. Being a good singer isn't enough to ensure success.

- Bob is quite tall and makes $10K more than his shorter friend, whose contributions to the company are similar. There is nothing in Bob's job description like "must be able to reach top shelves," so Bob knows he's being rewarded because the boss subconsciously thinks tall people are more capable.

Hahaha. Just kidding. Bob thinks he's making more because he kicks ass at his job.

We all know that good-looking people make more money than less-attractive people, and it's not limited to jobs like modeling or acting.

We don't need beauty to sell insurance or write programs

I've often thought we should celebrate sports achievements on an individual basis instead of in comparison to others. Maybe each runner should be awarded for beating his or her previous best time, for example. (I know this won't fly. I'm just throwing it out there.)

Let's think about female sex appeal.

Women who've got it may choose to flaunt it. Flaunting it, in some cases, can get you ahead.

If I'm a woman who can't flaunt it because I ain't got it, nobody wants to hear me complain, *"Well, Cindy just got that job because the boss wants to bone her."* Even in cases in which we all know it's true.

At some point, we decided people (well, women) with sex appeal should not use that to their advantage. Women who do so tend to be disrespected for it.

How can we defend this? Every other natural advantage people have is fair game, but women who are beautiful and/or sexy are not supposed to use that advantage to get ahead?

I call bullshit on that

Nobody should feel pressured or obligated to use their looks to get ahead, but nobody should be shamed for doing so, either. Everybody else is using everything they've got.

I'm dismayed, however, that female musicians are usually pressured to look sexy. Some women are happy to express themselves this way, but others are not. You should be able to depend on your amazing voice without having to show off your amazing figure, too. But musical talent being equal, the sexier woman has an advantage.

I'm 50-plus. When I was younger and prettier, I resisted the idea of capitalizing on my appearance in any way. Obviously, this gained me tons of respect and paid off in a big way.

Just kidding. Literally, nobody but me knew I was holding myself to certain standards, and I'd probably have gotten further in life if I'd used every advantage nature and the world had given me.

Where does all this get us?

I think when we're in decision-making positions we need to remind ourselves that the right person for the job might be loud and friendly or quiet and shy, or might be gorgeous or unattractive, or young or old.

Don't just pick people you like personally. That annoying person you can't stand might be the best person for the job.

I've seen hiring managers on LinkedIn state that they hire for personality, not skills. They say when they find the "right person" they can train them.

They don't seem to realize what they are saying is *"I will ignore people with a proven track record in my field. I'm looking for someone who seems like they'd fit into my social circle — somebody I'd like to hang out with."*

I have zero athletic ability

I was born with none, and no matter how hard I tried (and I tried *desperately* when I was in school) I couldn't develop any. I am inherently clumsy.

Others have natural abilities they enhance with serious practice. That's great for them. It doesn't make them better people, but it does make them better at athletics.

Every skill I can think of has two components: You are born with some inherent ability, but you also need to work at it.

In the end, I'm lucky to be better at writing than at playing sports.

The universe decided to give me some talent for writing, and I work hard at it. Being someone who can barely walk across the room without tripping is not much of an impediment to writing. Nobody requires writers to be young and beautiful.

I don't think anyone will ever say, *"You know, Michelle, we all loved your manuscript. It's genius — a real literary work of art. It's probably the best book any of us have ever read in our entire lives and it has the potential to change the world. However, there is a problem. We only represent hot women. You really should have submitted this when you were 18. You looked your best then."*

EVERY BILLIONAIRE IS MENTALLY ILL

My diagnosis? Pathological Money Hoarding Syndrome!

The Diagnostic and Statistical Manual of Mental Disorders is a delightful read.

I'm not joking.

My daughter is a therapist, and when she was finishing her degree, I purchased her first copy as a Christmas present. When I visit her, I love to thumb through the latest edition.

"Hmmm, this sounds like someone I know," I think to myself as I read the criteria for various disorders. I have secretly diagnosed almost everyone I know (including myself) with something.

It's like perusing Dr. Google and diagnosing yourself with pretty much every dread disease.

But the DSM requires a new addition: Pathological Money Hoarding Syndrome.

PMHS has many high-profile sufferers

While it's possible for a person of any income level to suffer from a pathological need to hoard resources, the more severe sufferers are billionaires.

It's possible to make millions in this world without having PMHS, but nobody becomes a billionaire without succumbing to it.

Let's think about normal human behavior, if such a thing actually exists. Let's imagine you're on an island and some disaster has meant there's little drinking water available. Everyone on the island is desperately thirsty. One man has tens of thousands of cases of bottled water – more than he would ever be able to drink in his lifetime. There's plenty to save everyone on the island, but the man who owns it refuses to give up a single bottle.

You'd consider him some combination of evil and crazy, right?

Why is it bad to hoard things like food, water and medicine but not money?

We don't admire people who hoard other resources

The men who stockpiled hand sanitizer during the early days of the pandemic were not congratulated as savvy Übermenschen. They were vilified, and rightly so.

It's odd that society admires the greed and decadence of those with PMHS. These are people who have enough money to meet all their own needs as well as the needs of their great-great-grandchildren and many generations beyond, but continue to amass wealth.

Many of them continue to ruthlessly squeeze resources from others

They will never be satisfied by their growing wealth. No dollar amount will be "enough."

It's more likely that an alcoholic will decide that the last beer they drank has quenched their thirst for all time than for a PMHS sufferer to decide to stop doing everything possible to amass more money.

Most of us have dreams of what we'd do if a fortune fell into our laps

I sure do. Like most of us, I'd want to provide some security for my family — but there would be no mansions or fabulous vacation homes.

Instead, the bulk of the money would go toward a foundation

I've always had in mind. My organization would provide a leg up for poor single moms. I enjoy imagining how I'd set it up.

Chasing pleasure is one of the quickest paths to misery. You get more joy and happiness out of accomplishing good things.

Could you enjoy cramming a sumptuous feast into your mouth while wide-eyed hungry children watched? Of course not. You'd feed them. You're not a monster.

You shouldn't have to actually be looking at hungry children to care about them. It's enough to know they're out there.

I'm not impressed by billionaires who hand out showy grants that gain them lots of publicity. It's not that giving money is bad; it's not. It's that there's something really wrong with anybody accumulating that much money in the first place.

Billions are extracted, not earned

It's hard to imagine that kind of money being made in an ethical manner. You can become quite wealthy earning money, but nobody "earns" billions.

I have never understood why the accumulation of more money than one can ever spend is any more morally acceptable than accumulating more food than one can eat or more medicine than you need … especially when your hoarding means others go without.

It's not only accepted, it's celebrated! Isn't that odd? There are those who truly admire billionaires.

Some billionaires have done some good things

I'm not saying otherwise. But they don't deserve to be viewed as superior human beings on the basis of their truly disgusting hoarded money.

For the most part, billionaires benefit from being in the right place at the right time. Most of them were born into families with some level of wealth that gave them a good launching pad in terms of money and connections. They had skills and a mindset that fit into the zeitgeist.

Had they been born in a different time or place, they'd be

ordinary laborers. I doubt they'd have distinguished themselves if they'd been born to a poor family, grew up in the developing world or lived 100 years ago.

Their hoarding harms others

When I hear about someone who is struggling in some way, I think, *"Gosh, I wish I could do something."* I bet you do, too. Sometimes you can find a way to help, but often the person has needs far beyond your ability to make a difference. If they're trying to raise money for medical care, maybe you could make a contribution but you probably couldn't bankroll the whole thing.

How does it feel, I wonder, to understand that one has enough money to solve the real problems of millions of deserving people yet choose to do things like putz around in space instead?

And it goes beyond the issue of charity

Once your empire gets to a certain size, it's easy to squeeze competitors in all sorts of ways. A small company trying to offer an alternative good or service at a better price for consumers will be bullied out. So the negativity doesn't just involve refusing to share one's wealth; it's also actively suppressing others' ability to earn their own.

These people have no shame, but that's not surprising, as they're treated like celebrities, not the hoarders they are.

The DSM does change over time as we better understand mental health. It removed homosexuality from the list of disorders in 1974.

Let's add in PMHS.

THE THING THAT KEEPS US POOR

How rethinking a cherished American ideal might help

A lot of us see being able to live in our own space as an important milestone. It sure was to me. When I was growing up I could not wait to move out.

I spent the summer after my freshman year back home with my parents, but after a taste of freedom, I found it impossible to return to living under strict parental rules and from then on I stayed in my college town all year until I graduated. I was thrilled to find a not-very-nice but extremely cheap basement apartment I could (barely) afford by working several minimum wage jobs.

I wanted to be free. Independent. Able to live my own way.

If my goal had been poverty, I could hardly have chosen a better way to ensure it.

In many areas, housing costs are through the roof

That's if you can even afford to have a roof over your head at all. In bigger cities, there are whole encampments of people who have jobs but still can't afford housing. Some people live in their cars and shower at a gym each morning before going to work.

But one has to wonder why several such people don't simply get a place to live together. If you live in adjacent tents or spend the night in the same parking lot, wouldn't it make sense to join forces? You'd have to share space but you'd be warm and would be able to shower and cook.

I didn't love having roommates, either. But if I had to choose between having roommates and living in a car or on the streets, I think that would be a pretty easy decision.

Is there really a housing shortage?
There is — and there isn't. Where I live, in central Illinois, there are plenty of nice and affordable houses in safe neighborhoods. People are not clamoring to come here. It's different, I know, in other parts of the country.

But even so, providing a single-person house or apartment for millions is far different from providing housing in which two or more people will live. If more than one person lived in most homes, we would need far fewer of them.

Ask a divorced parent about housing
When you go from two people putting their resources together to raise the children in one household to two people who are paying for separate households, the money just isn't going to go as far.

When the father of my children left our marriage in 2002, I knew I'd struggle financially. Most people do after a divorce. I tried to find another single mom with whom to share expenses. I had a nice three-bedroom suburban quad-level home and I knew I'd ultimately have to either sell it and buy something smaller or share space with someone else.

I thought two single moms could share expenses and swap babysitting. I even signed up for a service that matched single moms looking for housing and other single moms with a house looking for a roommate.

It was no go
A woman I knew in real life — a recently divorced Ukrainian lady with twin toddlers — decided to send her children back to Ukraine to live with her parents for a few years rather than put her kids in daycare. (I think of her often now and hope all her family is safe.)

I ended up selling the family home and moving to a

dramatically smaller and cheaper place in another town — one that I could afford as a modestly paid single mom.

I never liked living with roommates in college, honestly, but part of the problem was cramming strangers into a room about the size of a bathroom. I'd hoped that having a large enough space for everyone to have their own room would make that easier.

Think about what poor immigrants do

It's not uncommon for immigrants to band together to get a small apartment, the better to save up to start a business, bring over family members or send money home.

Many of these living conditions are far from ideal, of course. Having a dozen people in a tenement sounds and is horrific. But I suspect the willingness to take extreme measures — especially since they probably are a continent away from their extended families — is what allows some immigrants to launch businesses.

Americans don't like to live with other people

More Americans live alone than ever before. Plenty of people don't even want to live with a romantic partner. They prefer being single.

Just how much do people hate living with other people? Apparently, some people would rather live in their car, alone, than share an apartment with other people.

There are exceptions, of course. I'm heartened by the trend of students and older people joining forces. A person just starting out without much money moves in with an elderly person whose resources are growing thin. Both benefit.

I loved it when my son moved back home

He'd been living on his own, but struggling to pay his rent and student loans, for a couple of years. He was driving a beater. He moved back in, paid off his loans, started a 401(k), bought and paid off a good car and saved up enough money to furnish a new place and still have a good-sized emergency fund.

The key thing that made his return home work smoothly was he pitched in around the house, cleaned up after himself and paid his own personal expenses. My husband and I treated him like the fellow adult he was. You'd be surprised how fast your situation changes when you throw everything you would have put toward rent and utilities toward your debt and savings account instead.

More families should consider this, yet there is still stigma

People think there's something wrong with young adults living at home, and assume they're just sponging off their parents as they play video games all day. The old "guy living in his mom's basement" assumption gets old.

My son is in good financial shape now, but he might still be struggling if the only thing he could pay on his debts was the amount of money he'd have left after paying for rent and utilities.

Wealthy people can pay for their children's education and give them a car and money toward their first post-college home. For poor and lower-middle-class families, this is the next best thing.

This goes against the grain, of course

I doubt most Americans realize just how ingrained our feelings are about individualism, freedom and independence. We take pride in these attributes.

We don't question them.

However, there are a lot of ways to define "freedom," and a lot of ways to work toward your own version of it. My son's freedom and financial independence were built on the foundation of moving back home for a while.

Our refusal to consider even a few years of co-living costs us a lot more than we think.

In fact, I think we can say that it's our drive for freedom and independence that actually helps trap some people in poverty.

IT'S TIME TO BURST THAT BUBBLE YOU'RE IN

You can't see the world clearly from inside it

What in the hell is an average American — really?

Your mind immediately went to the people in your bubble.

You're thinking about the people you live near and work with. Your relatives. The people who go to your church or belong to your clubs. The families of the people your children are friends with. These, to you, are likely "average Americans."

You may have seen reports about the Wharton School of Business professor who asked her students how much they thought the average American wage might be. Shocker: They had no clue and most of them believed most Americans made very good wages. (A quarter of them thought the average pay was more than six figures!)

This explains how well-off people really do not understand why people like me are angry about … well, everything. Why am I complaining if most of us are making at least $100,000 a year? The system works wonderfully! We should all be ecstatic and completely satisfied with this capitalist playground we are all in!

You probably already know better

But well-off people are the ones running the world, setting policies and making laws. They are doing so without a clear idea of how most Americans really live.

I live in a gritty little working-class town, but there are well-off people living here, too.

For many years, I was the editor of what used to be a daily newspaper, and that gave me a look through the window into the lives of all kinds of people. I've had face time with local, state and national politicians as well as very poor people trying to live in unlivable conditions. I have friends who are quite well-off and others who are dirt poor.

I was a member of a community organization (dues paid by my employer) and as such had lunch once a week with local leaders at a country club, where I'd listen to people talk about very, very different subjects than the topics my poorer friends would discuss.

There was quite a bit of talk about upcoming vacations, for example, and taking multiple vacations a year was thought to be absolutely normal — because for them, it was. And almost all of those folks earnestly considered themselves middle class.

This isn't typical

Most of us stay in our bubbles and make wild assumptions about people unlike us. Several times, friends have unthinkingly suggested I make my life easier by enjoying a spa day or hiring someone to clean my house. They honestly couldn't imagine that someone might not be able to afford such a splurge.

I can 'pass' as privileged

I'm white and have a college education. I'm well-read. I know how to dress to fit in well enough when I want to.

But I always scrub my own toilets, make almost all our food from scratch and take some fairly extreme budget measures.

In some ways, I definitely am privileged — I've always had health insurance, and although I shop carefully, it's been many years since I truly worried about not being able to purchase enough groceries. I don't take any of that for granted.

What we need is some kind of exchange program

But instead of sending teens to live for a semester with people from another country, we'd assign people to spend meaningful time with people from different income levels.

The very first thing the well-off folks would notice is that lots of poor people are just as smart and hard-working as they are. I think the poor people would, in many cases, be surprised to see that many of the well-off people actually work hard, too. That's why so many of them honestly believe they are self-made people: It's not unusual for them to have put in lots of hard work and effort to get where they are. (They simply don't see that it's common for others to have done the same but not to have made any traction.)

In other cases, yes, the stereotypes hold true

There certainly are lazy poor people who have made incredibly dumb life choices that have held them back. There are absolutely well-off people who inherited a family business and have skated along ever since. It's a big country; there are lots of different people in it.

Have you ever watched two toddlers meet? In about five seconds, they're friends. They don't query each other about what preschool they attend and make judgments accordingly. They just start playing.

We adults are very careful about who we play with. Where do you work? Where do you live? We size people up and make sure they're bubble-worthy. We don't usually do this on purpose or even know we're doing it … but we do it.

Imagine how different our society would be if we didn't.

Sources:

Forbes
Wharton Professor Asks Her Business Students What The Average

American Earns—Their Answers Ranged Up To $800k
https://www.forbes.com/sites/jackkelly/2022/01/22/wharton-professor-ask-her-business-students-what-the-average-american-earns-their-answers-ranged-up-to-800k/?sh=5d01f2345784

LIFESTYLE CREEP IS OUT TO GET YOU

Will you ever be satisfied with what you have?

When I was in college, I often ate cereal with measuring spoons.

No, it wasn't some kind of crazy diet plan that required me to eat only 17 teaspoons of raisin bran or anything like that.

I owned one spoon and two forks and I didn't do my dishes after every meal, so that meant improvising a lot.

I coveted some ultra-cheap silverware with plastic handles at Walmart, but I was living on only $3.35 per hour and couldn't quite swing it.

Later, I got a set of hand-me-down silverware that was perfectly fine and served me for many years. But then I began to lust over the bridal-registry-quality flatware.

Oh, it was elegant stuff

My then-mother-in-law gave me a set for Christmas and I loved it so much. It was simple and understated; so much more stylish than the cheap set I'd had before.

And the plastic-handled stuff from Walmart? At that point, I wouldn't have taken it if you'd offered it to me for free.

I had succumbed to lifestyle creep

It happens to the best of us, especially if we started out poor. If you have very little money, you'll buy the most inexpensive sheets, dishes and other kitchenware you can find. You'll buy a dirt cheap lawn mower and vacuum cleaner, knowing they're junk that will wear out in no time, but hopefully not until you're in a position to replace them with better stuff.

You have to. The choice is to buy the low-quality item or do without it entirely. And you can't very well live without any dishes or sheets.

You know when you buy the thin-bottomed skillet that it's never going to work well. You wish you had a few more bucks so you could buy the heavy cookware your mom has — she's had her skillets for decades and they're still perfect. You plan to ditch your cheap skillet as soon as you can afford to get something better.

It's not that you don't realize you're paying a "poor tax." You know the money you spend on the cheap, crappy skillet is money wasted. You'd be money ahead if the first skillet you bought was a quality skillet you could use forever.

The same goes for getting a quality toaster. And a quality vacuum cleaner. And all the rest.

But you can't

However, you might be lucky enough to get fantastic wedding gifts or you might be able to wait to move out until you have a solid salary and can afford to buy quality goods the first time around. Even so, you're still susceptible to lifestyle creep:

- Did your last phone actually break, or did you just want an update? How about your computer? Your TV?
- Have you ever thrown out a pair of jeans that fit you just fine but were deemed too skinny or too high cut or too low cut by the self-appointed fashionistas?
- Have you ever sold a perfectly nice house to upgrade to a larger one with more amenities? Unless you had several babies, wasn't your old house large enough, honestly?

You think all the little upgrades and minor luxuries won't

amount to anything, but they can

Every so often, you read about someone like a janitor or librarian who shocks everyone by dying and leaving millions to charity. It's generally someone childless, living in an unassuming little bungalow, driving an older used car.

It's never anyone known for a flashy lifestyle

It's always someone who managed to live on just a little bit less money than they made.

But most people think they always need just a little bit more money to live.

"If I could find a job that paid me another $10,000, I'd be set!" people say. Then, if they do get that raise, they thriftily tuck it all into their retirement fund, of course.

Hahahaha! I'm joking. Of course they don't do that. They instead buy a fancier car or take a big vacation or upgrade their house.

And after they do that, you know what they say:

"Man, if I could just make another $20,000, I'd be set!"

ALL YOU GRATEFUL LAID-OFF PEOPLE ON LINKEDIN NEED TO GET REAL

WTF is wrong with you people?

When I was laid off from a job I loved — editor of my town's daily newspaper — I said nothing on social media for a day. I knew it was coming and had already been quietly taking home a few personal items each day, but the pain was intense anyway.

A day later, I was ready to post about it. I took the moral high road and didn't bad-mouth the corporation but I expressed my sadness at the end of my newspaper career, my pride in my accomplishments and my hope for success in another industry.

That's a normal way to respond to losing your job.

Do you know what isn't normal?

The bullshit I've been reading from laid-off folks on LinkedIn.

If you're on that platform, you've seen it.

Well, many of them did not *"lose their job,"* actually. They were *"impacted by the layoffs"* at their former employer. I keep seeing that phrase.

Why don't they want to actually say it? Why the euphemism?

Many of these folks are expressing their joy and excitement about the opportunities they are sure are just ahead. These people deny being sad about losing their job.

On the contrary, they are thrilled! They just know there are great things ahead for them.

Look, I hope there are. Sincerely! Being laid off sucks, especially if, like me, your expertise is something no longer in demand. It sucks even more if, also like me, you've reached an age at which it's very difficult to relaunch into a new career. Ageism exists, no matter what anybody claims.

Professionalism today seems to dictate psychotic levels of faux positivity

Why is this? Life has its ups and downs. There's no reason to deny that. No, you don't want to endlessly bitch or cry in public, but you also need not pretend that everything is wonderful when it's clearly not.

It doesn't make you seem positive, it makes you seem sort of psychotic. It's like the job equivalent to saying something like this:

"I was impacted by the death of my spouse of 20 years this week, and many of you have reached out to me, expressing your sympathy. However, I'm choosing to remember the amazing things we shared. I feel confident that there is another marriage out there for me, and after taking a quiet weekend trip to reset myself, I'll be out there looking for the next great marital adventure! #staypositive #available #opentolove

Or this:

"Now looking for our next #dreamhome after our entire neighborhood was demolished by a wildfire last night. We feel so lucky to have lived near so many amazing and inspirational neighbors, all of whom we will miss as we go on our next housing adventure. The best house for us is yet to come! If you have a great neighborhood you'd recommend, please feel free to reach out and touch base with us! #newhouse #newneighborhood #newlife

Admit it. That's creepy.

The relentless positivity hits me in the gut

I feel it viscerally.

I don't like anything fake — anything.

Think of a fake wood grain desk — wouldn't it be better if the designer embraced the fact that it's plastic and went with that, rather than trying to make it look like wood?

Real is always better, and real is not always nice. When something is not nice, you don't necessarily have to go into deep detail about how terrible it is, but neither do you have to fake that it's wonderful.

How to tell the world you have lost your job

Do not pretend you're happy, but don't say you've been crying and drinking vodka all afternoon, either.

Say you loved your job if you did, and express that you're looking for new opportunities and would love to hear from anyone who knows of openings in your field.

Yes, you can say you'll miss the people you worked with, if that's true. If not, don't badmouth anybody. Don't burn bridges.

Feel absolutely free to note the type of job you're looking for. Maybe you want to pivot to something slightly different.

If you absolutely cannot do that, here's another option.

You could always flame out

If you've pushed yourself too far into toxic positivity, perhaps you're ready to burn it all down, in which case you may as well make it worthwhile to everyone and write something like this:

Well, I was shitcanned by the losers at #Acme today. That bitch Susan in HR threw me under the bus just because she saw that one of my "friends" tagged me in some beach pics on social media after I called in sick with Covid.

The good thing is I will no longer have to watch my ass around that #asspincher Ron in accounting, but I'm sad that I will no longer have a cushy job with high pay or access to the primo office supplies I've been sneaking home for the last five years. (Those gel pens were the best!)

I am going to be taking some time off to enjoy my unemployment and hammer down shots of Jägermeister but in about five months I'll be looking for anything easy with high pay and great benefits.

Reach out if you can help! #officesupplies #unemploymentrocks #drinkinglikeagirlboss #acmesucks

It beats the fake positivity.

WORKERS ARE THE REAL PHILANTHROPISTS; BEZOS, GATES AND MUSK ARE JUST EXPLOITERS

Here's how the exploitation-philanthropy charade uses your money

I have two stained-glass windows in my parlor. One of them, I am told, was taken from the lovely old Carnegie Library in my town, which was torn down decades ago so we could build a boring brown brick box.

It's nice that Andrew Carnegie built 1,679 libraries across the U.S. But it's not nice that he built his fortune on the backs of men's lives. He worked them to death in his steel mills, literally in many cases, and paid poverty wages.

He exploited these workers and then, when he'd already enjoyed every possible luxury of his time, he started funding free libraries.

He was celebrated for this generosity

But each time I look at my stained-glass windows, I make a point to think of the exploited workers who paid for such beauty with their lives.

The real philanthropists were the workers, who toiled 12 hours a day, usually seven days per week, making Carnegie rich enough to give away millions.

We celebrate the wrong people

Jeff Bezos claims he's going to give away most of his wealth.

I have a better idea.

How about he pays his workers well instead? He shouldn't be a billionaire — the very existence of billionaires is disgusting. Nobody ever became a billionaire ethically.

If everyone in the Amazon empire made a decent and fair wage, Bezos would be rich but not a many-times-over billionaire.

The same is true of any number of companies that suck all the wealth for themselves, screwing over the people who make their wealth possible, and then, after a while, decide to crown themselves as philanthropists.

The Walton family's Walmart so sickens me that I've sworn off ever going there again. But realistically, it's nearly impossible to help enrich the exploiters.

The Bill & Melinda Gates Foundation does some good things around the world but a lot of not-so good things, too.

I'm all in favor of giving to others

Most of us do give to others in some way. Even those of us who have little money are generally happy to share a meal with a friend whose kitchen is bare.

We give the clothes our toddlers have outgrown to the neighbor with a new baby. We lend money to a coworker who needs it to buy gas to get through until payday.

Those kinds of routine philanthropy do not make headlines. Can you imagine?

Local Philanthropist David Carls Gives Major Gift
David Carls, owner of Dave's Speedy Lube Service, gave $25 out of his own pocket to one of his employees Tuesday, sources say.
"Ben just started here and was flat broke. He mentioned he was looking forward to his first payday so he could buy some groceries. He was down to one box of ramen noodles," said a man who asked not to be identified but whose clearly visible name tag read "Roger."
"When Dave heard that, he handed him some money and said, "Hey, this should help get you through the next couple of days. You're doing a good job and I'm glad to have you here."
At press time, Carls was refusing to confirm the story. "It's no big deal," he said.

We worship wealth

God knows why. It's just possible to become wealthy through hard work and paying your people well. It's possible to become a billionaire only through exploitation.

We all admire the people who started out poor, worked hard and built successful businesses. These people, of course, are extremely rare. There is little socio-economic mobility in the U.S.

If your parents were wealthy, you will probably be wealthy.

If your parents were poor, you will probably be poor.

The American Dream is hard to achieve if your parents were not economically successful. Here's a quote that says it all:

Economist Raj Chetty: "Your chance of achieving the American Dream is nearly twice as high in Canada relative to the United States."

Maybe we should start calling it "The Canadian Dream."

Barbara Ehrenreich died not long ago

I admired her so much. Her book *Nickel and Dimed: On (Not) Getting By in America* was genius. She took jobs all over the country as a housekeeper, motel maid, server and similar positions, and then she wrote about trying to live on her low income.

My favorite insight came from the last page of the book:

"The 'working poor,' as they are approvingly termed, are in fact the *major philanthropists of our society … they endure privation so that inflation will be low and stock prices high. To be a member of the working poor is to be an anonymous donor, a nameless benefactor, to everyone else."*

Yet these people are treated like crap

The people they enrich make splashy announcements about giving away money and are celebrated.

You saw what happened as a result of these people being given post-pandemic raises. Their privation lessened somewhat.

The powers that be have been doing everything possible to push these people right back into their place. We depend on them shutting up and working themselves to death.

I hope they refuse to do it.

Sources:

Office of Policy Development and Research
Economic Mobility: Measuring the American Dream
https://www.huduser.gov/portal/pdredge/pdr_edge_featd_article_071414.html

POOR PEOPLE AND RICH PEOPLE LIVE IN DIFFERENT WORLDS

But most people don't know it

A friend called me from the grocery store one Easter, mentioning she'd had to go to a different place than usual because her favorite store was closed for the holiday.

"I try to never go to the store on a holiday," I said.

She didn't understand why.

"Well, most of those people who came to work today probably would have preferred to be home. Maybe they wanted to drive to a relative's house for dinner or have an egg hunt with their kids. If nobody went to the store on Easter, they could be with their family."

"But they chose to be here," my friend said. "They get time-and-a-half."

"I'd be surprised if they did," I said. Though I've never worked in a grocery store, I worked a lot of service jobs as a student. Not once did I ever get paid extra for working a holiday.

Nor was I ever given a choice. If they scheduled you, you came in, or you were fired. That was that.

My friend was sure they were rewarded for holiday work

But with me on the phone, she asked one of the workers. Sure enough, the worker was not getting any special holiday pay. My friend was surprised by this. She talks to workers when she shops and thought she knew how their jobs worked.

The grocery store worker did say that it's possible to get a holiday off if you request it six months in advance, so it's likely that the more experienced employees are able to stay home and the newer people — those hired within the last six months — hold down the fort on holidays.

My friend never had to work a job at a grocery store. So she honestly had no idea, and how would she?

Leave it to me to bring these things up

My friend then said that grocery store workers chose to work there. They could have taken a different job.

"Nobody taking a job at a grocery store is choosing between working in the produce department or being a bank CEO," I said. Almost everyone working these kinds of jobs is working them because it's their best option.

It might be a mom who only works weekend shifts while her husband is home to take care of the kids, because they can't afford daycare, or it might be a student or someone just starting out in the work world. If they don't want to work in a grocery store, it's going to be some other kind of job with similar pay and requirements.

They don't generally have a better option because if they did, they'd take it.

My mother did work in a grocery store

Back in 1976, the factory where my father worked went on strike. It was a long, nasty, brutal strike that anyone my age and older who lived through it will remember well. I sure do, and I was only 10.

My mom had been home with my sister and me, but with Dad on strike, it was time for her to find a job. She didn't have any education beyond high school, so she started working at a grocery store.

She later was able to get a much better job at a food brokerage company, which was a smart move. She had a good salary, a company car and an early company cell phone. Her career was cut short by lung cancer; otherwise, there's no telling what she might have achieved.

As a student, I worked endless shit jobs

I worked at multiple restaurants, including several fast-food joints and one fancier place, where I cocktail waitressed. I worked in my college's food service and alumni office. (I also worked at the student newspaper, but for a tiny stipend significantly below minimum wage.)

I worked one summer at a factory that paid me $5 per hour, and I trimmed Christmas trees for two springs in a row for $4 per hour. Everything else paid me the minimum wage, $3.35 per hour. That was the minimum wage the entire time I was in high school and college.

Actually, I made an even lower hourly wage as a cocktail waitress, but the tips were decent. I made more as a lousy cocktail waitress than I did for many years as a pretty good journalist.

So I know my shit jobs. If there had been any way at all I could have landed a better job, I would definitely have gone for it.

If you object to me calling these jobs "shit jobs," well, I think I earned the right to call them what I want after working so many of them. I usually had more than one such job at a time, because I couldn't cover my living expenses with just one.

This explains why poor people suffer so much

The wealthy class doesn't send their kids out to flip burgers or stock grocery store shelves. They honestly do not know what these jobs are like.

If they spent one month living as a poor person, I would like to believe, most of them would immediately understand the reasoning for things like increasing the minimum wage, providing more affordable housing, instituting universal health care and many similar things.

It's not always that they don't give a shit about the working poor; they honestly don't understand what their lives are like.

The poor don't understand the lives of the rich, either

It's often assumed that every rich person has unlimited funds, which except in the case of billionaires is not true. It's assumed that every rich person inherited their wealth, which may or may not be true. It's assumed that rich people don't have big problems, which may or may not be true.

One of my friends thought anyone could have an overdraft removed

This person made an oopsie and overdrew an account.

The bank took it right off when they requested it. I had no idea such a thing was possible. The last time I overdrew my account was at least 20 years ago, but I remember calling the bank to no avail.

I took an informal poll of people I know. Most of us had no idea one could have an overdraft removed unless it was some highly unusual situation. Some of us had tried but had no luck.

I suspect banks are a lot more willing to remove an overdraft if you have a lot of money with them

They don't want to lose their good customers.

If I were to threaten to move my checking account to a competitor, they'd roll their eyes or maybe even fall onto the floor laughing.

"Sir, I must warn you — if you do not remove this $30 overdraft fee forthwith, I shall immediately take my $7.42 to another bank."

I am exaggerating a bit, but trust me, they wouldn't miss me.

Here's why this matters

Imagine you're a single mom with two kids and a poorly paid job. You have just enough money to pay your most pressing expenses as long as you do everything perfectly and nothing goes wrong.

Almost inevitably, at some point you overdraw your account,

even if ever so slightly. The $30 (or so) overdraft fee causes a cascade of overdrafts and overdraft fees, and before you know it, you can end up owing more in overdraft fees than you earn all week.

For someone teetering on the edge of homelessness, something like this can be the final blow. It would be nice if such a person could walk into a bank and have those overdrafts removed. And now that I know it's possible, I'd recommend people give that a try.

But based on the experiences of people I've asked about this, it doesn't sound like it's a successful request for most lower- or middle-class folks.

In other words, the people who could best afford an overdraft fee are more likely to be able to have them removed than the people who can least afford them. That's how the world always works.

It's expensive being poor

The best and most famous explanation of this is found in Terry Pratchett's book, *Men at Arms: A Novel of Discworld (Discworld, 15)*.

If you have somehow never read *Captain Samuel Vimes "Boots" theory of socioeconomic unfairness*, you are missing out and should at least read the quickie Wiki version. It's truly excellent.

I still think we need the income equivalent of foreign-exchange students.

I love the idea of foreign exchange students. You host a kid from another country and learn all kinds of things about the kid's home country. Or you live for a year in another country and come home with a lot of insights.

Now, let's do this with rich and poor people. Everyone *thinks* they know all about how other people live, but they usually don't. If you're rich, you completely discount all the advantages you started out with that made it possible. You may even claim to be self-made. You cannot understand why other people don't just make good choices, like you did.

About a week of staying with a poor family would blow your damned mind. There are reasons they make what look like poor choices to you. You'd quickly learn they don't have the same choices available to them.

As for the poor, they'd benefit from living with a rich family for a week

For one thing, they'd enjoy the break. But also, they would see that being rich isn't the same thing as having a perfect life. For the most part, rich people do need to work in some way, and some of them work just as hard as poor people do.

Having money is one thing; keeping it for the next generation is another.

'The Rich' and 'The Poor' aren't actually good categories

Everyone is different. And there's a big difference between the underclass and the working class. There's a big difference between the well-to-do and the 1 percent.

There are well-off people who got that way by hard work and there are others who got that way by being born into the right family. There are people who are poor because they've made poor choices and others who were hit with challenges they found it impossible to overcome.

But still. We'd all be better off if we got out of our bubbles and really got to know people living different lives.

Sources:

Wikipedia
Boots theory
https://en.wikipedia.org/wiki/Boots_theory

I WONDER WHAT ALL THE POOR PEOPLE ARE DOING TODAY?

Probably working their asses off

Many years ago, a friend won the free use of a boat for a day. She invited my family and her sister, a very poor single mom, to cruise the Illinois River with her. None of us was remotely used to such luxury. It was awesome.

The sister, who took a day off from her grueling work as a nursing home CNA, settled back on a cushy seat and said the words that still crack me up today:

"I wonder what all the poor people are doing today?"

All Americans are rich, some people claim

Around the world, about 710 million people live on less than $2.15 per day, according to World Vision. You've heard it said that Americans (and other Westerners) are all wealthy.

Why would a single mom raising two kids on less than $20,000 per year complain? She's a bazillionaire compared to her sisters in the developing world!

That's bull and I can prove it

No, the American poor are not rich. That's a GOP talking point.

Traditionally, we considered food, clothing and shelter to

be basic needs, but Americans today need what I will call "soft necessities," without which they can't pay for the "hard necessities" of food, clothing and shelter.

You need a job to pay rent, and you need decent grooming to get a job. So yeah, being able to pay for a basic haircut is necessary to avoid homelessness.

A lot of things people consider extras are actually necessities in today's world

My husband and I have more than enough food and clothing. We even own our shelter. But in order to keep our house, my husband and I need to make enough money to cover the cost of keeping a car. Other than in large cities with public transportation, most Americans will need a car to get to work.

So is car insurance a necessity? Well, yeah. Because without it, we can't drive our car, which would mean my husband could not get to work, which would mean we would lose our house. (I work from home.) Car maintenance and repairs are necessities, too.

Are computers and cell phones necessities?

I was well into adulthood before I had either. Couldn't I save a little money by doing without them?

No, I can't. I need my phone and my computer — and my internet service — to earn money, without which I would not be able to continue paying for other basic necessities.

My water, sewer and garbage costs are in the neighborhood of the total income of those folks who subsist on $2.15 per day. At one time, these costs did not exist. You dug a well and built an outhouse. You burned your trash.

My parents did pay for trash pickup when I was a kid, but they didn't pay a dime for their water or sewer. We had a well and a septic tank. We did have to keep our electric water pump running and once we had to have our septic tank pumped out, but I'm sure that added up to far less than the monthly bills we all pay now.

Free water and sewer are not options for any American now other than those living in remote rural locations. Nor can you simply burn all your trash. We could revert to the old ways, I suppose, if we like cholera and smoky air.

There are any number of things that are, today, necessities. You cannot be a functioning member of society without paying for a whole lot of these soft necessities.

Shampoo, deodorant, freshly laundered clothing in decent shape, a halfway presentable haircut — these are soft necessities because without paying money for them, most jobs are not open to you, making it impossible to pay for hard necessities.

You pay a price for doing things yourself

My husband doesn't get this at all.

He wants to do everything possible himself. He designed and built our deck furniture by hand, for example, and it's awesome. But if he had granted himself even minimum wage, it might have been cheaper to have purchased a set.

Not everything has to be based on cost, of course. He enjoys making things, and everything he builds is of better quality than we could have purchased.

But it's worth remembering that your time has value

I have washed my laundry by hand at various times in my life. It's possible. But it's quite time-consuming.

I actually do a lot of things by hand that most don't, like hand-washing my dishes and hanging up my laundry to dry, but all that stuff takes time away that I could otherwise be using to earn money, so there's a trade-off.

We purchased a new washing machine when our old one died. That's worth it to me — but buying and operating a dryer is not. Everyone will make decisions about where to draw that line depending on their own time and money calculation.

Childcare costs are unbelievable

My daughter has two children. At one point, I realized her weekly summer daycare cost was more than I have ever earned in a week in my life!

It's absolutely not optional. If she doesn't pay for childcare she can't work, and she has to work.

If we lived closer, I'd be glad to watch my grandchildren for free. They aren't so young as to require constant hands-on care; I could still get a reasonable amount of work done if they were here.

However, it would take some time out of my day in order to care for them properly. You can't just park a kid in front of a TV and ignore them all day, even though some poor people have little choice but to do just that. And then we wonder why their children are behind in school. Hint: It's not because they are stupid or don't know better. It's the way we've set up our society.

It was a college English professor who taught me the real purpose of money

I remember her saying two memorable things in class.

One related to writing: *Padded writing is like a padded bra. Both are ultimately a disappointment.*

One was just an aside that really struck me: *The purpose of having money is to avoid hassles in one's life.*

I don't consider myself poor right now, but I've never had enough money to avoid hassles.

The lower your income, the more hassles you face

If you're poor or poor-adjacent, you're probably driving an old car, and car repairs are an enormous hassle. Newer cars don't break down as often, but poor people can't afford them.

I can remember days when something like a broken fuel pump meant calling around and seeing what friend knew how to replace it and begging rides to work until that friend could get to it.

By comparison, life is great now: I can have an actual mechanic fix it. I aspire to have a car that is new enough that I can realistically expect few car repairs.

That time is not now.

Similar hassles fill the days of poor and poor-adjacent people

It's stressful because every problem has to be solved creatively when you can't just throw money at it.

Here's a perfect example. We need some foundation work done

that will require steel beams. We reduced the cost a little by using scrap steel we got free from my husband's workplace. Also, I got a slightly better deal on the foundation work because I do SEO for the foundation people.

That's how it works for the poor, the working class, and some portion of the middle class.

It's all or nothing in the U.S.

Sure, if you want to live under a bridge and panhandle, you can survive on very little money. But once you fall to that level, you may never be able to climb up again.

Once you can't afford to bathe, trim your hair, dress decently, get a cellphone for callbacks and pay for transportation to work, nobody is going to hire you. People standing on the lower rungs of society can see this abyss clearly and are terrified to lose their grip. They understand how important it is to preserve their place in society.

If they cannot pay for the soft necessities, they have very little chance of paying for the hard necessities.

I'll tell you what the poor people are doing today

They're doing the same thing everyone except the very wealthy is doing: Worrying.

Sources:

World Vision
Global poverty: Facts, FAQs, and how to help
https://www.worldvision.org/sponsorship-news-stories/global-poverty-facts#:~:text=Mostly%20through%20household%20surveys%2C%20they,population%2C%20lived%20in%20extreme%20poverty.

THE DARK SIDE OF HEARTWARMING STORIES

What's really going on here?

I keep reading stories that are supposed to pull on my heartstrings but are instead pissing me off.

The formula goes like this: Person faces something bad. Person needs help. Savior comes through. Everyone wipes a tear.

The real story often goes something like this: A person is facing something bad because our system isn't set up very well. Society declines to address the problem. Savior comes through.

Everyone is so used to things sucking that they don't even notice the crucial fact: We should fix the things that are wrong in our system because we don't have enough saviors to come through for everyone.

You've read some version of all these:
- A kid with cancer needs treatment his or her family can't afford. The kid's family and friends throw a benefit to pay for treatment, and thanks to a caring community, they manage to raise the money the kid needs.
- Another one: A worker who is ill/has a child who is ill runs out of sick days, but the worker's caring co-workers contribute their own unused sick days.
- Then there's the one about the poor man who, someone realizes, is walking very long distances to work each day. The

savior pops up, raises money to get the guy a car, and everyone cheers.

I invite you to think about these things:
Kids (and adults!) with cancer or other serious illnesses should have their medical treatment covered. People who are sick or whose child is sick shouldn't have to beg colleagues for sick days — their job should offer this benefit.

Why are we so heartless as to make people who are already in crisis have to deal with such things?

'Spot charity' is a problem
Everybody loves the story of the deserving poor person being rewarded.

That's because people accept the narrative that poor people are poor because they're lazy and stupid. Some poor people *are* lazy and stupid. Some rich people are lazy and stupid, too. But most people are trying.

A newspaper in my area used to do a series of stories about needy local residents going through hard times. The series raised money for a fund that the paper used to purchase holiday meals and toys for struggling families.

Here is what always struck me about those stories — most of them were people caught up in situations beyond their control. Quite a few of them focused on families whose struggles dated from the birth of a child with significant medical problems who needed a constant caregiver and often an expensive mix of medications, therapy and surgery.

That sort of thing could happen to any family, and the fix for that is universal healthcare.

It's not as if people don't care
If I were to tell you that your next-door neighbor is a Type 1 diabetic who just used her last vial of insulin and who has literally no money at all to pay for her next dose, and asked you to please contribute so she could stay alive while she tries to deal with her crappy insurance company, I am absolutely positive you would

give it if you had it.

If you learned your cousin is walking 10 miles to and from work each day and is exhausted and developing plantar fasciitis, and you had an old car you scarcely ever drove, you'd probably loan or give it to her.

If a hungry child came to your door and asked for a sandwich, you'd feed him, right?

I doubt I'm wrong about this

Most of us are more than willing to provide a little help if it's within our power to give it. Now, all we have to do is recognize that there are millions of people among us who do need help and that if everyone contributed a little bit, we could make their lives much better or even save their lives.

There are some awful people in this world, but I can't think of anybody I know who would actually turn away a hungry child or refuse to help someone whose life depended on being able to purchase insulin.

That's kind of how universal healthcare works, of course. We all pay some taxes and the help is there for everyone who needs it. The same goes for food benefits.

It feels a lot different when there's a specific hungry child at your door than when you're asked to pay taxes to help cover the cost of feeding kids you'll never meet.

We've been given all sorts of reasons to believe human kindness is actually bad

Nobody says it's bad to feed a hungry child. Instead, we are offered these alternative facts:
- The government isn't really helping these people; it is making them dependent on the government.
- The government isn't really helping these people; it's wasting tax money on fraud and corruption.
- The government is punishing hard workers by taking their money and giving it to lazy moochers.
- The government shouldn't have to feed a kid. Where are that

kid's lazy parents?

I'm always surprised by how willing people are to help a specific person they can see, and how unwilling they are to pay money that is supposed to help people in general.

Perhaps this has to do with our evolutionary past.
For most of human history, we lived in small bands, and we knew every single human in them very well. If someone was suffering, we generally knew why. Our hunter-gatherer ancestors did share things with each other, but they also did expect everyone to contribute — and it would have been obvious when someone wasn't pulling their weight.

We seem to need to see a face to really care. That's what's behind all the social media posts seeking contributions for some deserving needy person.

The trouble is, not every needy person makes a heart-warming social media post
Sad, big-eyed children look more appealing than bedridden elderly people who cannot interact.

That guy sleeping on the sidewalk who irritates passersby — what's his origin story? If he was a decorated combat veteran who developed PTSD while serving his country, we should probably give that poor man some help. But if he's a schizophrenic who smells bad and panhandles, we better keep moving along and avoid eye contact.

It becomes a popularity contest. The people with a compelling story get help. The others don't.

We cannot fix every person's problems individually
But we can fix the system, if we care to. We'll have fewer heart-tugging stories on social media, but I can live with that

'DIRTY HANDS, CLEAN MONEY'

The guy with that bumper sticker and I should start a new political party

We were both speeding down the highway, but if we had been walking across a parking lot, I'd have taken a chance on talking to the guy with that bumper sticker.

I'd have liked to have talked to him about the way everyone depends on the working class to make and fix things, yet the monied class disrespects them.

I felt like we could have cautiously had a beer together.

Over that beer, we could talk about the value of honest labor. And maybe, just maybe, he'd agree with me that the rich are sucking the lifeblood out of the poor and that workers need strong unions again.

He might stop nodding and smiling once I said we've all been worse off since President Ronald Reagan deliberately started dismantling the middle class. Maybe I could win him back if I quickly blurted out that we all want the same thing here — to be able to support our families decently and to live our lives freely.

But by some of the other stickers on his car — eagles and flags — I suspect he'd have abandoned both me and his beer by the time I started talking about the dangers of former President Donald Trump. Eagles and flags are great, but just now their presence tends to signal less savory associations. (I'm really sad to say that, too.)

I'd listen to the guy's thoughts

I don't know anything about that one particular man, but I grew up in a tiny town and I live in a red area. My dad was a Boilermaker at a factory for decades. I often talk to conservatives.

So I already have a fairly good idea of what he'd say.

He would probably tell me he's tired of being called a racist when he's not. That he personally knows lazy people who get welfare when they could be working. He would tell me that kids who run up student loans to get college educations deserve their debt because they could have made more going into the trades. He would say that America is the best damned country in the world and that if I don't like it, I can leave it.

He would not be impressed by any statistics or background I would offer. The conversation would probably not end amicably.

That's the reason we don't talk: We all hate each other now.

I blame our two-party system

Two parties are not enough. We should have half a dozen. We're a big country, and we have a lot of different people. Two parties doesn't begin to serve us all.

I have learned a lot from my Dutch husband. Take a look at the wild collection of political parties in the Netherlands! Wow! They have tons.

There are so many — and they have to form coalitions with each other, because you're never going to have just one party hold all the power.

They have to find some other parties they have some views in common with and get along at least until they've passed some kind of legislation they all want.

If we had a bunch of smaller parties, that guy's party — we couldn't call it the Workers Party, so maybe the Dirty Hands Party — and the Democratic Socialist Party could get together to boost unions. They would come together for that vote, but would part ways, perhaps, when it came time to pass a vote protecting LGBTQ people and abortion rights.

But that would be OK, because the Democratic Socialist Party and the Human Rights For All Party and maybe the Green Party would work together to pass LGBTQ and abortion rights.

They'd need to work together, because the Proudly Fascist Boys Party would be in bed with the Christian Party, both of them working to destroy human rights for all but straight white Christians.

Remember when the feminists got into bed with the Christians to attack pornography? (The worst sex ever, no doubt!) Regardless of how you feel about that, it proves the old saying that politics makes strange bedfellows.

If we had multiple parties, people with wildly different political views could come together on some issues and then part ways on others. Stuff would actually get done.

As an extra perk, it would be harder to hate the other side when they just helped you pass one particular bill you were able to agree about.

Our two-party system isn't working

The Republicans are trying to stuff traditional Christianity, big business, small business, banking and finance, the military-industrial complex and the anti-tax and anti-civil rights people all under one gigantic tent.

Hardly anyone is a true Republican. If you split the party into one that focused on Christianity and another on money, everybody in the two new parties would be happier. (Call it the God and Mammon split.)

It's the same with the Democrats. They would certainly be happier if they were split into a couple of different parties.

We have the Tea Party and the Libertarians and the Greens already, but they can't get anything done because they're not part of the two main parties. Most people won't vote for a third party, because as things are, it always hands power to the "other side."

Votes for a Green candidate probably cost Democrat votes and hand victory to the Republicans, even though Green voters most likely prefer a Democrat over a Republican.

Similarly, votes for a Libertarian probably cost Republican votes and hand victory to the Democrats, even though Libertarian voters most likely prefer a Republican over a Democrat.

For this reason, the two main parties have a stranglehold on everyone, even though most of us have to hold our nose to vote.

I've said before that nobody 'earns' a billion dollars

That kind of money is not earned; it's extracted and extorted. Billionaires have clean hands and dirty money. The guy in the truck would, I think, have a decent level of agreement with me on that matter.

We'd probably agree on a few more things if we didn't feel forced into opposite camps.

IT'S JUST MONEY, PEOPLE

Why do we allow it to take our lives?

Occasionally art tries to remind us that money is worthless, but we never pay attention.

There's a scene in *The Road* when the man is walking through dust and litter that includes utterly several worthless $20 bills. Remember when the police officer in *Fargo* notes that people were killed for something so inconsequential as money? More recently, Jimmy McGill is asked toward the end of *Better Call Saul* if he did all the terrible things he did just for money.

Money has 'value,' but no inherent value

If you and I were starving in some dystopia and then you found a secret source of food, you would not accept my offer of a million bucks for it.

I guess you could start a fire using a $20 bill. Or maybe you could melt down coins to make a tool. But most money today is only digital, so you don't even have that. Imagine trying to explain to someone a hundred years ago that you work day and night for money that you will never even see, let alone touch.

The value is dropping all the time.

You can buy stuff with this virtual money, but in times like right now, the money is losing value due to inflation. Just think of how hard you worked to earn money that is now worth less than it was when you earned it.

Under the barter system, maybe I'd give you a chair I'd made in exchange for some of your wool. And you know what? We'd both have something tangible. Not now.

I carry a small amount of actual money with me for emergencies

But I don't carry very much, and you probably don't, either. I can sort of understand the appeal of having a chest full of gold coins hidden away, but for most of us, our money doesn't even exist.

Almost everything earned in my household is direct deposited, other than one agency I freelance for that mails me paper checks for some reason. I pay most of our bills online. After I use my credit card to pay for something, it is paid off each month automatically by my bank, using the money that someone has sent us digitally.

The only time I have a sense of having bought something is when I go to a store, swipe my card and bring home groceries or plants or a pair of shoes.

But for the rest, I don't see the money when I earn it, and I don't see the money when it goes off automatically to pay the mortgage, the utilities, the credit card and the insurance. It's like it never existed.

For this, my husband and I work our asses off.

I don't want anything, but that doesn't matter

We have built a society that requires everyone to work very hard even if they don't desire wealth.

Even if you are unmoved by desires for a mansion, yacht and jewels, you'll probably have to keep working well into your old age. You need money in reserve, because you don't know how long you'll live or if you might become ill and need expensive medical care.

You could have half a million (virtual) dollars in the bank, and still be legitimately concerned about what will happen to you if you need to enter a nursing home someday.

People are working harder than ever now

Not everyone, of course. The top 10 percent or so are doing fine.

But isn't it crazy, for example, that young moms who have just given birth — even when they have a working partner — are expected to put down their newborn and drag themselves back to work? They'll be expected to do all the work they always did, even though now they have to attach a pump to their breasts to collect milk and use a sanitary napkin to catch the post-partum bleeding. This, they must do just to have enough money to take care of their baby.

How about all those seniors you see working in fast food or as cashiers? I will never forget the woman I saw working while on oxygen. Why was that older lady not at home resting, for God's sake?

Fear of being one of those seniors someday is another reason why the new mom is trying to work at her computer while the double pump under her shirt collects her milk.

Have we gone insane?

We have created enough damn wealth

If you live in the U.S., look around you. There's so much money in this country, but little of it goes to the workers. Most of us get far less than we deserve for the work we do. Let us keep a little bit of it to live — to really live.

Because while money is just a social construct, our lives are not. Our lives truly exist, yet we devote them to work. And for what? Mostly, not for our own benefit.

Yes, we are insane.

DOES POVERTY BUILD YOUR CHARACTER?

What if you already have plenty of it?

My son got his first job at 13. It was hot, dirty, exhausting work detasseling corn for a local ag operation.

Removing the tassel from the top of a corn plant doesn't sound so hard — until you think about the sun burning your face, the sharp leaves of the corn plant cutting and irritating your skin, the mud sucking at your boots, the mosquitoes eating you alive and the fatigue of your muscles from repeated motions. Heat stroke deaths of teenagers doing such work are not unheard of.

Each afternoon, my son would call me from a phone at the grocery store where the farmer dropped off the crew, and I'd pick him up. He'd be hot, muddy and exhausted, the tips of his ears always somehow burnt despite his sunscreen and hat.

A lot of kids quit after the first day

But he stuck with it and made enough money in a few weeks to pay for a computer, which had been his goal.

When I told him the job was good for his character, he sardonically asked why I didn't join him out there and get some character for myself.

"My character was formed many years ago," I told him. "I don't need any more of it." And in truth, the newspaper job I had then was another character-building experience of long hours, heavy responsibilities and light paychecks.

You know, I have enough damned character

A woman I know with a trust fund opened my eyes to how the 1 percent live. And I'll tell you one thing, they don't send their kids out to the fields to detassel.

They don't seem to worry about their kids' character suffering from a soft life. They focus more on getting their children into good schools and moving in the right circles.

The whole "character" thing is bullshit we've all been sold to keep us working. And each time anybody in my class admits that they resent working hard for little money, having difficulty paying their bills, or wanting more time with their family, they are immediately shot down by the owner class as being lazy and entitled.

It's ingrained in our society

I think back to a woman I knew years ago who told me about a landlord illegally kicking her and her young children out on the street. The experience was horrific, and yet she said it did her a favor: It made her fearless. She knew she could survive anything after that.

There's something to be said for knowing you can handle hard times.

When the pandemic hit, some people panicked. I did not. I was prepared. My pantry was stocked. I bought N-95s a year before the pandemic.

I never take it for granted that things will be fine. On the contrary, I expect trouble at every turn.

I'm often not wrong.

The toxic positivity people love to claim that we can manifest great things just by imagining them, and that we should believe the universe will provide for us. I imagine if you could see a Venn diagram of people who live in poverty and people who believe in this theory, the circles would not even touch.

It's a superstition for rich people, nothing more.

What I would like is for hard work to pay off

I bought into the idea that hard work, thrift and a willingness to find resourceful ways to make the most of things are virtues that pay off in time. It should not have taken me so long to realize all that was just a line fed to the bottom half to keep us quiet.

We shouldn't be quiet anymore. We should speak up about the need for unions, universal healthcare, subsidized child care and affordable or free higher education. We should speak up about the need to make it possible for ordinary people to meet their basic needs.

Ignore the people who will complain that we're entitled and lazy. That's just how they try to shame us into not asking for what we deserve.

Besides, note that other industrialized countries manage to do all those things much better than the U.S. does. Note that it's generally the Republicans who resist implementing these things, and vote accordingly.

It's astonishing to me that the GOP is successfully positioning itself as the party of the working class. Nothing could be further from the truth.

The working class as a whole has plenty of character. What we want now is our share of the wealth of the world. We have already earned it, and we aren't asking for charity when we demand it. We're just asking for what we are owed.

WE'RE STILL HERE, SO THERE'S THAT

There can be more, though

You had dreams.

Maybe some of them came true. But if you've read this far, you probably feel you're missing something. Not everything is right, even if some things did work out OK. And if you look around the country and around the world, there is so much stuff that's wrong.

Why? Doesn't everyone want things to be better? Aren't we all doing our best? Why have we made such a mess of things?

So here we are, you and me. I'm writing this, and you're reading it, because we both can't help but think things ought to be better than they are.

I'm easy to find online, and I'd love to continue the conversation.

Michelle Teheux
https://michelleteheux.medium.com
https://substack.com/@michelleteheux

ABOUT THE AUTHOR

Michelle Teheux

A former newspaper editor, Michelle is a writer on Medium.com and publishes a Substack newsletter about income inequality called Untrickled. She has two children and two grandchildren. She and her husband, Harrie, live in a small town in central Illinois.

PRAISE FOR AUTHOR

The Trailer Park Rules
Americans have a problem with poor people: they don't like them.
We make assumptions about why a person is poor, assuming they're lazy, they're stupid, they made bad decisions or they just like living in a constant state of deprivation, fear and insecurity.
The Trailer Park Rules, by Michelle Teheux, offers up the stories of a dozen residents and visitors at Loire Mobile Home Park. The trailer park stands in for any low-income housing, whether it be subsidized housing or barely appropriate living quarters on the "other side of the tracks."
Each chapter of the book showcases an individual character, allowing each character's past to unfold and their future prospects to appear.
These are interesting characters, mostly people you come to care about. Each time I put down the book, I looked forward to getting back to it, hoping to see some folks get their comeuppance and hoping others get a happy ending.
Teheux has written a book that is enlightening, as well as a fun read. There is humor, compassion and surprising twists.
Take some time to know the folks at Loire Mobile Home Park. You'll enjoy it and maybe think about some preconceived notions you might have brought with you.

- L. BROWN

I read this in one sitting. The character development and page turning story telling... all while highlighting the very real issues that face working class people, make for a fantastic read. It's quite the social commentary.

It was also sad because I could so relate the stories of the trailer park, er, excuse me, MOBILE HOME park residents. Being a resident in a mobile home park myself, I am watching with horror as big corporations swoop in, buy up smaller family owned parks, jack up the rents... and leave a wake of displaced families. This includes the handicapped and elderly.

I urge you to read and join in a conversation about the need for affordable housing for all.

- THERESA WINN

"The Trailer Park Rules" is a riveting, poignant, often funny, ultimately surprising take on class, media, race, sex and the way people on the economic fringe of society interact as they do what they must to survive.

The structure of the novel, divided into chapters named for a rotating cast of characters who become increasingly familiar, draws you right in. The story meanders just enough to feel culled from real life, before finally all coming together. Lots of little twists — and one big one — keep the pages turning.

The best novels create and introduce us to new worlds (or in this case, a world we knew existed but had never lived in).

Having never lived in a trailer park, I went into the story with a few hackneyed stereotypes in mind but little else. By the time it was over, I felt like I'd lived there, among these people — admiring some of them, others not so much, but with the sense that all of them were real.

It's been a long time since I've burrowed into a book that had me anxious to get back to it at the end of each day. This is a great read that both entertains and makes you think.

- KEVIN MCDERMOTT

BOOKS BY THIS AUTHOR

The Trailer Park Rules

All wealthy families are alike; each poor family is poor in its own way.
— Leo Tolstoy, if he had written about a trailer park

For residents of the Loire Mobile Home Park, surviving means understanding which rules to follow and which to break. Each has landed in the trailer park for wildly different reasons.

Jonesy is a failed journalist at a dying newspaper with one dream left. Angel is the kind of irresponsible single mother society just shakes its head about, and her daughter Maya is the kid everybody overlooks. Jimmy and Janiece Jackson wanted to be the first in their families to achieve the American dream, but all the positive attitude in the world can't solve their predicament. Darren is a disabled man just trying to enjoy his life despite a dark past. Kaitlin is a former stripper with a sugar daddy, while Shirley is an older lady who has come down in the world and lives in denial. Nancy runs the park like a tyrant, but finds when a larger corporation takes over that she's not different from the residents.

When the new owners jack up the lot rent, the lives of everyone in the park shift dramatically and in some cases tragically.

Made in the USA
Monee, IL
22 October 2024